How to Teach Junior Highs

Books by
BARBARA SMITH
Published by The Westminster Press
How to Teach Junior Highs
Young People's Bible Dictionary

HOW to TEACH JUNIOR HIGHS

by

Barbara Smith

Philadelphia

THE WESTMINSTER PRESS

PUBLISHED BY THE WESTMINSTER PRESS ®

PHILADELPHIA, PENNSYLVANIA

PRINTED IN THE UNITED STATES OF AMERICA

Contents

1. Can Junior Highs Be Taught?

The Teacher Looks at the Pupils

TEACHING MORE BUT ENJOYING IT LESS

H.W.C. (He Who Has Been Chosen) has just closed the front door after lengthy good-bys to the pastor of his church (or the chairman of Christian education or whoever has the job of interviewing prospective teachers). It seems they want him to teach a class of junior highs. H.W.C. goes back to the living room, picks up the paper, then puts it down, and begins to think over the interview that has just taken place.

Perhaps H.W.C. said no. "No," he said firmly to the recruiter, "I couldn't handle kids that age." Thinking it over now, he adds to himself, "Everybody knows they don't have any discipline; they just run wild. No, sir, not me!" And he is sure that he has exhibited great wisdom in refusing.

Perhaps H.W.C. agreed to take the class. Now he is wondering about his wisdom, whether he has any or not. "I don't envy you!" says his wife. She tells him what Mrs. Jones said about the class she taught last year and the experiences of the Browns, who were advisers to the Sunday evening fellowship for a few months. As news gets around the church that H.W.C. is to teach in the junior high department, he finds that a great many people agree with his wife and Mrs. Jones and the Browns and the H.W.C. who wanted to say no.

The teacher-to-be is invited to sit in on several classes before starting his work. In all these classes he finds that coming late is the custom. In one class he observes that there is a brief wrestling period among the boys before the teacher gets order and starts the lesson. Another teacher spends ten minutes in conversation about yesterday's game in the canny hope, H.W.C. perceives, that he can retain the interest of the young people in the lesson when it begins. The girls in another class are more or less openly passing wallets around and looking at snapshots while the teacher drones on. In another group every junior high seems attentive. There is no obvious disorder, but everyone has slightly glazed-over eyes. H.W.C. bets himself that their thoughts are a thousand miles away. When the teacher asks a question his hunch seems to have been right. H.W.C. gets a strong impression from his visits, an impression of disinterest on the part of the junior highs and earnest attempts by the teachers to secure interest.

H.W.C. goes to one of the regular meetings of the junior high staff. He finds that the meeting quickly turns into a gripe session. The teachers say: "I have to work hard to make it interesting." "They're more interested in sports." "I find it difficult to put some of this stuff across." "They talk by the hour about school, sports, the other kids. But they clam up when I try to get them to talk about the lesson." "How do you get their interest?"

Then H.W.C. goes to another kind of meeting. It is for teachers from several churches, and an "expert" is on hand to answer questions. Right away a woman in the third row says, "I want to talk about discipline!" And H.W.C. hears again how kids this age have no respect, are hard to handle, are not interested. The questions seem to boil down to, "How do you get the attention of junior highs?" H.W.C. thinks the teachers mean to ask, "How do you get them interested in a subject that doesn't seem to be of interest to them?"

The prospective teacher is keeping a cool head, for he

does have wisdom, in spite of his doubts. He sees that there is a sort of truce prevailing in junior high classes, a truce between the disinterest of the pupils and the attempts of the teachers to make interesting a subject that at heart they consider of no interest to young people. Neither side presses the conflict with zeal; the white flag is always flying. The junior highs have little choice about being there. They are resigned to it, and their disinterest takes mostly indirect expression. The teachers blame the pupils (i.e., ask about discipline), or blame themselves (i.e., ask how they can make it more interesting), or blame the material (i.e., complain that it's too hard).

Without a cool head, H.W.C., when he starts to teach, will fall into the same trap of conflict and truce. Thereafter, he will enter into disillusionment, depression, even despair, about teaching in the church. Such is the unacknowledged state of many a teacher of young adolescents, a state of teaching more but enjoying it less.

The imaginary experiences and observations of H.W.C. and the estimate of his possible future have been somewhat exaggerated, but not much. Check them out with your own experience. Find the persons in your church who are responsible for getting new teachers. Ask them what reasons are most frequently given by those who refuse to teach junior highs. How many people have you heard say, "I could teach children but not young people"? Why are young people considered harder to handle?

You may never have seen any class in action except your own. Perhaps in your class there are no noticeable signs of disinterest (it is possible to avoid them). But if you could observe in other classes, you might see many such signs. As a substitute for observation, listen to the common complaints of teachers. Do they match or resemble what H.W.C. heard at the teachers meeting? How frequent are questions of "discipline" at teachers meetings? What experiences lie behind such questions?

Do any teachers you know *say* that junior highs are unteachable? Do any teachers you know *think* that junior highs are unteachable or act as though that were the case? Do you agree or disagree with H.W.C.'s observation that there is in many junior high classes a state of truce in a continuing conflict? If you feel this is not true in your class, to what do you attribute the difference?

Warning: Many a teacher is blinded by his conviction that something *ought* to be of interest to young people. The teacher of the junior highs with glazed-over eyes may not know that his pupils are bored. It is possible that the teacher of the wallet-passing girls does not even see what is going on.

THE VIEW FROM OUTSIDE

The conflict situation that H.W.C. shrewdly observed stems from an all-too-common approach to teaching young adolescents in the church. It is based on adult views of adolescence, views taken entirely from the outside. Young people are "they." "They" can be, and are, characterized in various ways.

The common, over-the-back-fence comments of mates, friends, and fellow church workers on the subject of teaching young people will reinforce the view from the outside, sometimes adding a note of fear. For the views that society in general holds about adolescents today are external, having to do with "them."

The teacher who indulges in some training—whether by reading or by going to teachers meetings or courses—will find that the popular external approach is further reinforced by what he learns. His book or his course usually starts with "what makes junior highs tick," or the characteristics of young people. From here he may be encouraged to search out some of the numerous books, pamphlets, and films that describe the growth processes, characteristics, and interests of the age group. (Most of these sources describe later adolescence. Information about the transition from late childhood to early adolescence is rare.) These resources about adolescence are helpful, and the conscientious teacher ought to study them. However, too often, either by his trainers or by his own deductions, the teacher is led to suppose that his work consists of matching the observable interests of young people and the resources of the Christian faith.

Some teaching programs are based on such a sensible proposition. As an extreme example, material about Jesus Christ has been used to help young people know how to be friends by considering Jesus and his friends. The observable interest here is the concern of young people for getting along with others. A piece of Bible material was selected to meet and guide this interest. But the Bible material was distorted to a purpose for which it was never intended.

What more frequently happens is that the teacher, trained in and wedded to an external approach, distorts the resources of faith (all on his own, while his teaching materials suggest something else) in an effort to make the subject of interest. He looks for an interest of junior highs and then, willy-nilly, tacks on something about Christian faith.

The way of the external approach leads eventually to the truce between pupils and teachers that H.W.C. found. When teaching is based on what can be observed from the outside about young people and their interests, it takes only a short time for the teacher to reach disillusionment. He quickly comes to believe—correctly, within the limits of the basic proposition—that the Christian faith is a subject extraneous to the interests of young adolescents which has to be forced on them or to which they must be motivated.

What are some typical, over-the-back-fence comments about junior highs and adolescents in general? What do your neighbors say? Do you find in such comments any evidence of fear? Such as?

What things are usually listed as characteristics of young people? Recall some or find a typical list. What would you assume about the interests of junior highs according to what you hear them talk about (outside of class time, that is)?

How common is the idea that teaching the Christian faith consists of matching the interests of young people and the resources of faith? A variation of the idea is expressed in the definition of church school teaching as "meeting the needs of young people." What needs are implied in this definition? Perhaps you have an entirely different idea of teaching. How would you contrast it with the external approach?

WHAT THEN?

With disillusionment in getting the interest of young people begins the disintegration of any possibility of teaching. The teacher is beset with problems that he identifies in various ways.

Some teachers will locate the problem in "young people today" and complain that they are hopeless, so different from what the teachers were when they were young. Or they will find the root of the problem in parents who are not bringing up young people in the right way (meaning, presumably, a way that will make it possible for them to listen to the teacher). Or the world we live in and evil forces in it may make it impossible for teachers to get anything across. Such teachers think that discipline will make young people pay attention to something they ought to be learning.

A certain type of teacher becomes a collector of tricky, showy methods, gleaning them from other teachers, from the preacher (especially from the children's sermons), from Bible bookstores, from proven sales techniques. Anything "different" in his teaching material, he supposes, is a technique for getting interest.

Another teacher may wrap himself in his own interest and simply not see that the pupils are disinterested. He goes blithely on, listening to himself with interest and therefore not needing to ask, "Is anyone listening?" So long as the pupils are quiet and orderly, all is well. Even when they aren't, the teacher may settle for the fact that his class is out of hand. He hopes that something he says will fall on their ears in the intervals of silence.

Still another kind of teacher tries to effect a compromise. He starts the session with a period of conversation about what the junior highs are interested in. The pupils respond and converse with spirit, also sometimes with tongue in cheek, for they know what is going on. Talking about their activities is the orange juice with the castor oil of the lesson that will follow. Driven to an extreme, this type of teacher abandons all teaching and just talks in a friendly way of this and that. The talking may touch on a "problem," giving the teacher an opportunity to drag in a "lesson" (junior highs will take that kind of honest view of the matter). He will seldom know that he has heard nothing at all of what interests young people. Many pupils in his class will complain bitterly about the treatment they are getting.

Suppose the teachers in the four cases described were allowed to voice their problems in a meeting. What questions do you think each one would ask? Imagine that you are present at the meeting and, along with other teachers, you try to answer the questions of the four. What would you suggest in each case?

Alert readers will have picked out some inadequacies in the teaching methods of these four types of teachers (as well as in the classes H.W.C. observed). Which do you think is the case: That certain methods to which teachers cling incline them to take an external approach? Or that the external approach in general leads toward the use of certain methods?

One of the cases above suggests how junior highs will react. How do you think they would react in the other cases? What might they say to their parents about their class? What might they say to each other about the class and the teacher?

A COMPLICATING FACTOR

There is in the air nowadays a generalized fear of adolescents that intensifies the common external approach in church school teaching. A straw man has been set up by easy journalism, by popularized psychology, by the grapevine from parent to parent, by our fondness for easy categorization. The name of the straw man is, usually, "Teen-Ager." The word has gathered enough doubtful connotations that some young people resent being labeled "teens" or "teen-agers." The straw man need not take the form of a leather-jacketed youth to conjure up a fear of adolescence. Average parents of average boys and girls often wait, tensely braced, for the first signs of the terrible teens.

Of course, the straw man was not constructed from nothing. Everyone knows that there is a wide gap between the generations, between young people and adults. A number of factors in our time have doubtless contributed to widening the gap. What do we tend to do when faced with a minority group that is different from us, whether in color or faith, economic level or neighborhood? We call them "they," we generalize about them, we keep them separate and at a safe distance from ourselves, sometimes only in the ways we think about them, sometimes also in our actions. It seems we have fallen into a similar trap in thinking about "teen-agers."

There may be a number of explanations for this phenomenon to which few thinkers have addressed themselves. Some feel that the major adult values of getting and spending do not allow for the seeking, questioning, independent nature of adolescence. Plagued by the need to conform, tuned in endlessly to the right things signaled to us by our neighbors, we do not want to have around us the unconforming individuality or the unconforming group life of adolescents. A little reflection on these tense, non-adolescent-admitting attitudes of society today may suggest the rather adolescent nature of them. Are not teen-agers supposed to be the best conformers of all? It is as though we fear to open ourselves to the reality of the adolescent stage of growth because we might recognize that we are, after all, barely grown up ourselves.

Deeper possibilities are suggested. One has to do with our time as an era of changing sex standards. The adult generation is the one most strongly caught between, on the one hand, old patterns of marriage and old sex taboos, and on the other hand, newer ideas of the family group and greater sexual permissiveness. Adolescents, coming as they do to an age of strong sexual interest, stir old guilts and conflicts in adults. Such stirrings find expression in unconscious but strong feelings of rejection, although they usually take forms that seem to have no relation to their source.

Yet another depth source of the fear of adolescents may be at work, one that has to do with hope. How many adults hold any genuine hope about the meaning and future of the world? The "hope" of building a new family-room wing on the house next year or even the "hope" of getting Johnny into college—these are the "hopeful" substitutes that keep us from experiencing the hopelessness we feel. Over against this prevalent but unacknowledged condition of our time, consider the growing process of the adolescent to whom the future is all-important and whose middle name must be hope. What kind of challenge does he present to the adult world? How can adults react to this molecule of hope except to stamp it out of existence one way or another?

Here and there, chiefly in the minds of advertisers and journalists, the straw man has been extended into a youth culture. Advertisers seem to think that adolescents and their money (of which they have considerable) can be parted more easily by the appeal of "everyone's doing it," and by widening the gap between young people and parents, who might otherwise have something to say about the use of the money. Presumably, journalists find the concept a ready source for articles. What is to be said, however, for church youth workers who have accepted this theory? For it unquestionably reinforces the tendency to look at adolescents as "they."

What are the characteristics usually attributed to the straw man, Teen-Ager? Why do young people object to the label and the characterization?

In your own experience, do you find evidences of a fear of adolescents in general? If so, what specific evidences have you noted? Perhaps you do not agree that such a fear exists.

How do you assess the three possible explanations given here: adult values, changing sexual standards, lack of hope? What other possible explanations would you suggest?

Why would it be peculiarly inappropriate for church workers with youth to be consciously or unconsciously infected by a fear of youth?

OTHER DIFFICULTIES

So far, the charges against the external approach to teaching are: that it leads to continuing suppressed conflict, that it produces teachers with problems, that it can lead to distortions of the Christian faith.

To these should be added the wide gap between the pupils and the teacher that exists from the beginning but rapidly becomes a conflict of interests. "They" are to grasp an idea that the teacher possesses and is eager, yes, anxious, to present to them. The teacher, as a representative of the church, of parents, and of the adult world in general, holds out to the young people something that is good for them. Unwittingly, he thus allies himself with the wrong side of the necessary conflict adolescents go through in loosening the ties with parents and home. It is difficult to see how the teacher, having put himself in such a position, can even understand his pupils.

The common approach to teaching takes itself altogether too seriously because it is obligated to be good for young people. The more fear of youth that prevails, the more this is true. Teachers are then put under pressure to preserve at least these few young people from the terrible fate of becoming adolescents. It is an easy step from something good for youth to the setting up of goals—things to do or not to do which the young people are to carry out Monday through Friday in school, and every day at home. However, every young person has observed that the "oughts" are not put into practice and are often used by adults to cover up whatever they want to do. He feels that the adult is trying to put something over on him, which may be the case.

The external approach considers "religion" as one area of life to be balanced along with many others. Since this is a widely held view among adults, it is no wonder that it is followed in teaching young people. But doing so means accepting as a premise of teaching a rivalry among interests in which "religion" nearly always loses. The complaints of teachers often reveal that they accept the fact of the battle, if not of the defeat. Why else are they driven to make teaching so "interesting"?

Bored and dissatisfied junior highs might be added to the list of complaints. The most frequent one that young adolescents make (to outsiders, rarely to their teachers) about their church school classes is that "we never do anything." They talk over frankly the evasive tactics they use, while wishing that they did not have to, and criticize themselves for not getting down to business. However, the business they want to get to may not be what the teacher has in mind, for they also criticize their teachers for not getting down to business either. Therein lies, perhaps, one of the main charges against the common external approach to teaching in the church. It never seems to get to the heart of the matter. Junior highs sense this; teachers ought to know it.

Keeping in mind the basic characterization—starting with the observed interests of junior highs from an outside view and matching them with resources of the Christian faith—do you think these charges against the external approach are true or untrue? fair or unfair? accurate or exaggerated? important or beside the point?

LOOKING AT JUNIOR HIGHS

H.W.C., at the time he was asked to teach, knew a few of the pupils in the class he was to take. He was acquainted with two of them through knowing their parents. A few others he had seen around the church. According to the comments of acquaintances, he should be prepared to classify them all as "difficult." But he was not willing to do so.

When he observed the class in action, he noted first the great variety among the junior highs, a variety different from that in a group of adults. Some were tall; some were short. One would find differing heights among adults. But also, some had childlike bodies, whereas others had more mature bodies and were obviously growing. A few seemed almost like adults. The girls, he noticed, tended to be more mature in figure than the boys.

The prospective teacher's second impression was of considerable physical vitality. Each young person had an irrepressible store of energy. The teachers he observed seemed bent on having the junior highs hold in their energy, but each pupil found a way to let some of it out. This one wriggled; that one tapped a foot. Another played with a pencil; one rubbed his face and pulled an ear. One pupil, in answering a question, sent forth words like steam from an engine.

Once H.W.C. started to work with junior highs, he was able to make observations of other kinds. He became acquainted with voices and mannerisms. He learned that this one spoke slowly and hesitantly, seldom able to find the words to express his numerous ideas. That one blurted out words when he had no ideas in his head at all. Another was so shy as to be nearly speechless. A few wanted to take the lead constantly, impatient of anyone slower than they. Some liked to be asked questions and to discuss; others seemed to wait for H.W.C. to talk to them. A few were slow at reading; a few were rapid readers. All these things and others H.W.C. noticed in classwork.

He got acquainted with the parents and brothers and sisters of the junior highs. He talked with their teachers in order to find out what they did in school. He made the acquaintance of the adult leaders of clubs and activities in which the young people took part. Occasionally he went to games and events such as the science fair in which his pupils were participants. He also planned some get-to-gethers and outings for the class that were different from the Sunday morning session.

In addition, the new teacher read all he could find about adolescents and especially about young adolescents. Sometimes what he read checked out with his own observations. Alongside some of the descriptions he put question marks. He amused himself by making small graphs with decidedly up-and-down lines in the margins of the books. These were his private reminders that, while a certain description might be true in a general way, the junior highs he knew varied, exhibiting more or less of a certain characteristic.

H.W.C. had a hunch that he, at least, might avoid ending up in a truce with the young people if he refused to accept common judgments of them. Instead, he planned to keep an open mind, to observe constantly, to add this bit of observation to that, to question his own conclusions as well as those of others. He wanted to know these junior highs for himself.

Yet the new teacher felt there remained a wide gap between him and his pupils. They remained adolescents and he remained an adult. It was clear that the junior highs were intensely absorbed in becoming adults—and that they were not adults. H.W.C. could not go back to being an adolescent again and meet them on their level. Indeed, he did not want to recall having been there. Where was there any meeting point between them other than the situation in which H.W.C. was supposed to interest them in something that interested them not at all?

Underline or make a list of the different things H.W.C. did to get acquainted with the junior highs in his class.

Do you think his observations will help him avoid the trap of looking at young people only from the outside? Why or why not?

Do you feel he should be more a friend to junior highs and less an observer?

Attention, detectives! A clue to the way out of H.W.C.'s problem is given in the above section. Can you find it?

LOOKING WITHIN

What H.W.C. has to do now is to stop looking at the junior highs and start looking at himself. The block he may shortly face is his reluctance to stand where his pupils stand and to see life, momentarily, as they see it. Once he can do that, he will learn things that the comments of neighbors and fellow workers, the books on adolescence, and all his observations will not make known to him. He may see that young adolescence looks rather different from such a point of view.

The gap between youth and adults comes about because of the reluctance of adults to recall what it was like to be adolescents. The adult forgets those years, mercifully and necessarily. The maturing person draws a veil over memories of his youth. According to his adult standards, the things he did then were foolish, wasteful, aimless, altogether shameful, and painful to remember. Recalling them threatens the person he has become. His inability to look back is not a simple matter of forgetfulness; it is charged with feeling. The situation is different when it comes to remembering himself as a child. Childhood memories are safe and precious because the painful, feelingful ones are completely concealed. Memories from adolescence have not been so efficiently censored. Consider just two aspects of these memories, sexual interest and rebellion against parents, and it is clear why they cannot be readily recalled.

It is this protective veil which so often separates parents and their adolescent children. Few parents can afford to recall that they once did and were all the things they now complain their children do and are, and yet lived to become reasonably mature. Not only so, but adults often do not want anyone around who may threaten to make them remember. The same protective veil, much intensified, underlies the fear of adolescents in society today. It has much to do with the fact that many people prefer to work with children rather than with young people. And it is a major factor in the inability of many adults to work with youth except on the basis of a truce.

However, what stands between the adult and remembrance of his youth is only a veil. The adult who can draw it back will find that the internal view of adolescence is rather different from the external view.

What he recalls may or may not match the characteristics and growth goals described in the books about young people. According to them, memories of adolescence ought to be comprised in large part of the trial-and-error process of having close friends of the same sex and the intensified trial and error of making friends among the opposite sex. Another large category of memories should consist of feelings of growing independence from parents and homelife. The remembering adult does bring to mind occasions that fit into these two main categories. He is usually surprised by the intensity and the integrity of the feelings he had on such occasions. Is it possible that the young people he knows have such sensitivity? Do their feelings have integrity also if one stops viewing them merely as threats and annoyances to adults?

Beyond the incidents of adolescence, the remembering adult recalls an inner level of thinking and feeling that surprises him, partly because of its subject matter, partly because of the remembered intensity of it, and partly because he has completely forgotten it. He may remember writing poetry or wishing he could. Looking back, he may see that he spent an amazing amount of time in daydreaming about the future. It was quite possible then to sit and contemplate great things like the universe and the meaning of life or to pause in wonder before something beautiful. Most of these inner concerns, he finds, seem to have been big, "philosophical," experimental, highly impractical, according to his present, adult way of looking at things. Do young people today think such big thoughts? Is it possible to concede the integrity of their thoughtfulness if one looks at it from another standpoint than that of adult values?

The great advantage that comes to the remembering adult is that he sees an essential difference between adulthood and early adolescence. The difference lies in the presence and consciousness of an intense inner life of feeling and thinking. Even adults live chiefly out of the resources of the inner life, but they tend to lose touch with it. They are more preoccupied with the external, sometimes to the near extinction of their inner lives. Thus adults tend to size up adolescents in the same way, externally. In doing so, they reject as unreal and unimportant the inner life of young people.

The remembering adult will also perceive that what happened to him, what he did and thought and felt, belonged to him alone. No one living now, no one yet to be born, no one in the past, could have his particular, individual experiences and his reactions to them. Thus, he does not use his own past as a guide to the exact experiences any young person today will have. Instead, he uses it as a corrective to generalizations about youth and to tendencies to characterize young people as "they." He sees that each individual adolescent has his own inner life about which no one else knows. The remembering adult cannot find his youthful life relived in anyone else, not even in his own children, although many parents try to do so. But he can stand alongside of and understand the inner life as the essential, real life of youth.

The inner life of young adolescents is not readily observable by looking at them or even by listening to them. Eavesdropping on a conversation of depth among a group of young teens, the adult may catch the serious, probing intent of the wildly sagacious-silly comments. But, by and large, the ponderings of junior highs are concealed from adults because they know that few adults will take them seriously. Adults seem to be finished with the question of the meaning of life; they prefer that no one around them should trouble himself or them with the subject.

The temporary nature of the inner thoughtfulness of adolescents, evidenced in the forgetfulness of adults, does not change the importance of it to the growing person. Its value is the same as that of play to the small child, a means of intense learning that is discarded or changed in later life. Adults give the child freedom to play, and enjoy the fact that he does play. They are more hesitant to give the adolescent freedom to think and to dream, and tend to react strongly to his doing so.

Most people cannot readily recall themselves as young adolescents. However, it is worth a try. You can start by remembering the most important thing that happened to you when you were twelve, thirteen, or fourteen. How did you feel about it then? Do not be surprised if your recalled feelings make you slightly uncomfortable now; that is why you have difficulty remembering. Try this in a group of teachers and consider how your inner memories match with what you observe about young people. Then consider whether young adolescents have similar experiences and feelings. Or are they, perhaps, "different" today?

A better way to recall is to do so through the memories of others in fictional or autobiographical descriptions of adolescence.

THE FOUNDATION FOR STUDY

Many teachers of young adolescents could benefit from conscious recall of their own young lives. However, it is not possible or necessary for everyone to do so. More important is the recognition that the basis for teaching young adolescents is the inner life of feeling and thinking, with its "philosophical" concerns, its probing, questioning, pondering, concluding, and then starting the whole process again.

Adults who guide junior highs in study will be those who set aside adult-slanted convictions about the nature of youth and enter into the inner life of young adolescents as it is and as most adults recall it was. Not that adults should attempt to become again what they were then; such a thing is impossible. But they can be adults who take with seriousness the inner life of junior highs. They will be adults who can and will listen to the ponderings of the inner life. Which is not to say that they will or must agree with the views of youth. But they will not reject such views on the grounds of an adult evaluation of them. Nor will they point out to youth the temporary nature of their thoughtfulness in an attempt to hasten maturity.

Furthermore, materials and the approach to teaching will be directed toward the inner life, not toward interests or needs. Such a foundation for teaching can get to the heart of the matter, which evades both pupils and teacher so long as they are engaged in a conflict of interest. Such a foundation cannot be equated with observable interests. It cannot be ranged alongside them as one more interest; it is life itself.

Study consists of bringing together the inner life of young adolescents and the sources of information that we have about faith.

You have taken one step in considering the nature of study concerned with a basic understanding of young adolescents and of what is teachable within them. Before proceeding to Chapter 2 and the next step, consider your reactions to the foundation for teaching suggested here. Does it seem to you sound or shaky? likely to make teaching easier or more difficult? different from an interest-based approach, or the same but deeper?

Warning: Resist the temptation to make a profile of the inner life of young adolescents or a list of characteristics. Why is this not possible?

2. How Firm a Foundation?

The Teacher Looks at Theories of Christian Education

Indignant Teacher, commenting on the idea set forth in Chapter 1 about the basis within young adolescents for study: "Nonsense!"

Which, translated, means:

That's a mighty shaky basis for teaching something eternally true and right. It's just a phase that young people go through. We had better find some more solid foundation that will last a lifetime.

More solid foundations are available: they can be found in the many current theories of Christian education. Theory, it is commonly supposed, is abstract and impractical, the exclusive concern of high-level Christian educators. The teacher at the grass-roots level claims that he deals with practical reality and is theoryless. In fact, however, every teacher has a governing idea behind his teaching, although he seldom thinks about it or develops it as a formal theory. A skilled observer can usually reconstruct the teacher's guiding idea by watching him teach.

Christian education theories in the formal sense underlie curriculum materials. Sometimes the teacher's own idea is influenced or added to by the approach taken in the materials he uses. Sometimes the individual teacher's theory and the formal theory differ from each other. All teacher training courses present theories, whether explicitly and formally, or implicitly in what they teach about methods.

Before reading further, try putting into words your own idea of Christian education. This is your theory, although you may not be able to express it as a theory. Write some key words and ideas on a slip of paper, then tuck it away and take it out again after you have read the next section.

A HALF DOZEN THEORIES

Supposing that a number of teachers could tell about the theories they hold, here are some of the things they might say:

MRS. STEP-BY-STEP, who has read current books about Christian education and attended training courses:

"One thing I have learned is that teaching is based on the stages of growth the person goes through. You don't have to teach everything at once. At the junior high level, for example, you can count on certain things that the pupils learned in the junior department or in primary classes, or, even, in kindergarten. These previous learnings are the foundation on which you build. You base your teaching on what young people of junior high age can understand—what they are ready to learn at their present stage of growth. At senior high level, they will go farther, building on the foundation laid at junior high and earlier levels. A word that is often used for this process is 'nurture.' I like the term because to me it means guiding growth in the Christian life just as one guides the natural growth of a child."

The developmental approach to Christian education is probably the most popular of current theories. Teaching faith, according to this view, is like setting building blocks on top of each other. Elements of faith are taught one by one, each resting on the previous one, making eventually an edifice known as the Christian life. Teaching materials based on the developmental approach set forth in clear dimensions the building blocks to be used at each age level, as well as the blueprint for building. The step-by-step emphasis makes it necessary to characterize each age group rather definitely. Teachers and theorists who hold this point of view are anxious to do things in the right order, to avoid introducing advanced building blocks at an early age or slipping in a block that may have to be taken out and replaced later.

MR. ALTOGETHER, a pastor who holds a six-week church membership training class for junior highs:

"There are certain fundamentals of the faith that these young people must know. I am constantly amazed that they come to my class, that they have reached the teen years, not knowing basic things they should have learned long ago. In my opinion the teachers of little children give too much time to play and to "frills," and neglect to lay a foundation of faith. You know, the Roman Church says, 'Give us a child until he is six . . .' and he will never desert the faith he is taught. They know what they're talking about. Every year in my church membership class I have to make up for what wasn't done earlier. I select questions from the catechism about the important points of faith. Together with the Creed and certain Bible passages, these make a program of memory work that each young person must master before the end of the class. Young people know something when they leave my class."

This approach pays no attention to development, but is based on the ability of the mind to memorize. Faith, according to this idea, is a solid, unchanging block of information to be learned and relearned and relearned until it is fixed, and thereafter "applied to life." Teachers holding this view are usually anxious that children should learn everything early in life. A developmentalist would say that such teachers tend to overteach in the younger grades, that is, to aim beyond the ability of the children to understand. At older levels, they usually underteach. Drill, review, and memorization are the favored methods in this approach. It is often adopted by those preparing junior highs for church membership in line with a tradition that certain things must be learned before one can become a communicant member.

MR. PERSONALITY, an average teacher:

"The purpose of Christian education is to produce Christians, in other words, people with Christian character. As I see it, character is a matter of attitudes and actions, which are the result of learning. The Bible tells us what we ought to do in the Ten Commandments and in Jesus' teaching that we should love God and our neighbors. Young people should learn the great principles found in the Bible and how to apply them in their own lives. We have to teach them good habits and desirable traits, such as honesty, purity, regard for others—in short, the way to live like Christians."

Training Christian character is the aim of this approach. It is based on the conviction that faith is supposed to make a difference in how the believer lives and acts. The "difference" is defined in a certain kind of character and in certain actions that are to result from learning. Teaching programs and procedures in this approach are based on the possibility of opening a compartment in a person, like honesty, and filling it with attitudes and principles. Thereafter the pupil is supposed to review the principles he has learned before he acts in that area. "Changed lives" is what teachers and theorists in this school of thought look for. The existence of character traits has been questioned for a number of years, yet a well-known formal theory of Christian education is based on the possibility of training them.

MR. INTELLECTUAL, a minister employed by a denominational board of Christian education:

"The outcome of Christian education should be Christians who think theologically. What do I mean by that? First, let us see that everyone has theological thoughts:

everyone thinks about God. Most people's thoughts are vague and uninformed, or wrongly informed by many influences around them. Theology, on the other hand, has very exact words and concepts. The church's theology is an accumulation of the faith of our fathers. It should be our aim to teach children and young people the words and concepts of theology so that they have a clear understanding of faith. Then they will be equipped to live in the world as people who know something about God. They will be able to assess and to correct vague and wrongly informed ideas. Yes, this means hard work. It means using the mind and coming to a disciplined understanding. After all, it is reason that controls our actions."

The intellect offers a solid foundation for other Christian educators, mostly professionals. Here the key word is theology, the knowledge of God. People who hold this view wish to implant early the words and concepts of theology, which they believe will be clues to life experiences later on. Because theology has been in vogue among intellectuals these past few years, the approach has attractions. The ability to "talk theology" attributes status in some church circles. Many teachers find it satisfying to be challenged to delve into a difficult field and to become "lay theologians."

Miss Inspiration, a professional worker with a non-denominational youth movement:

"In my opinion church teaching today is far too intellectual. It is cold and lacks feeling. What we need is some of the warmth and fervor of the old-time religion, an appeal to the feelings. This is especially true of young people who are experiencing many new, strong emotions that should be channeled into spiritual expressions. Every young person should have an experience of Christ. Too many people are allowed to join the church although they have had no real experience of faith. In my work I regularly give a call to young people to come to Christ and be saved."

Rare today, but still to be found, is teaching that finds its sure foundation in the emotions. At first glance, it seems to be the direct opposite of the intellectual, theological approach. Many of its practitioners are undyingly suspicious of thought in any form. Yet the emotional approach is grounded in the same dualistic psychology as the intellectual one: a view of the person that divides him into opposed faculties of reason and feeling. Adherents of this view seek for "experiences"—an experience of Christ, a salvation experience, worship experiences, mountaintop experiences. Few teachers, except those of the nondenominational Bible story hours and youth crusades, hold this view exclusively. However, it is always likely to appear in the teaching of young adolescents. According to an old tradition in the church, the emotions are ripe at that age for "commitment," another key word for emotionalists. People who ordinarily hold other views of teaching will lapse into this approach when it comes to questions of "joining the church." They will urge young adolescents to have "experiences," and to make lifetime commitments on the basis of them.

MRS. CITIZEN:
"Christian teaching builds on the foundation of the home. It is really an extension of what all good parents teach their children from the beginning—common decency, the ability to live life successfully. In the church, of course, we are especially concerned with helping people learn to use the resources of religion to meet life's problems. I think of my work as being close to that of the public-school teacher also. Our subjects are different, but our methods and aims are the same. We are both concerned with training the minds and abilities of young people so that they can be good citizens ready to take their places in the world. The church adds spiritual values and motivation to what both home and school teach every day."

For people like Mrs. Citizen there is a firm foundation in the similarities between Christian education and all other kinds of education, especially that of the schools. For many years church schools have been measuring themselves against public-school work. Perhaps, in terms of methods, it is right to do so. Perhaps it is also right to wish to make church school teaching as reputable as the public-school teacher's work, so that it can command equal respect. Education in general, because of its position in our free society, holds that faith is "religion," one interest among many that make up the person's life. The usual view of educators is that religion is useful in inculcating morals and spiritual values. The more education feels that it is responsible for the whole child, the more educators wish to rely on the outside agency of religion to give character training a motivation they cannot give it. (In a similar way, some governmental and superpatriotic views in recent years have held that the purpose of religion is the formation of national character.) Church school teachers and theorists who follow the leads of education often consider their work in the same terms, as a supplementary arm to general education.

With which of these approaches to Christian education do you find yourself most in sympathy? Which do you dislike most and why?

How would you describe your own idea of Christian education? Take out that piece of paper on which you wrote your theory. Is it like one of these? Made up of several of them? Entirely different from any of them?

Each theory has behind it a certain psychology or view of the person. See if you can outline some of the main points of each. On what part of the person does each theory base itself? Compare these with the basis suggested in Chapter 1. If you are talking over these questions with a group of teachers, your discussion may lead to nothing but confusion. However, the confusion can show two things: The flimsy bases of opinion and half knowledge of most of our ideas of Christian education. The need for some further learning about people and how they operate.

Each theory implies a certain view of what faith is. See if you can describe each, then consider how adequate you find them to be. In discussing this with others, you will find there are as many views of faith as there are psychologies. Don't run the discussion into the ground. In fact, it would be a good idea to cut it off at its warmest point and send everyone out for a cup of coffee or on to the next section of this chapter.

THE UNANSWERED QUESTION

The individual teacher's theory of Christian education has its source chiefly in tradition, that is, in how and what he was taught, which was how and what his teacher was taught, and so on into the past. Christian education theorists—denominational executives, curriculum planners, and others—use other sources, although tradition has been known to enter into their theorizing also. They usually employ insights from the fields of psychology, theology, and education. They take care in deciding which psychology, which theology, and which educational theory or method they choose, because each field of knowledge includes many schools of thought. They also use these three fields to correct one another, and try to strike an acceptable balance among them. Most Christian educators are trained in one of the three relevant fields of knowledge, sometimes two, rarely all three. There is, therefore, considerable controversy at high levels. Clearly there is enough work to occupy theorists for many years.

"What is man?" "How do people learn?" "What are the stages of growth?" "Who is God?" are the questions Christian educators ask. These are all good questions; it is helpful to know answers to them. But in the midst of all this questioning and choosing and balancing stands the individual teacher who, if he has begun to be thoughtful, asks another unanswered question, "What is faith?" Even a slight acquaintance with the many theories of Christian education shows that each has a different view of faith. Is faith the sum total of all these views, a many-splendored thing? Can tradition, psychology, theology, and education be sources of information about faith? Each of them, with the possible exception of education, will claim that it can. Each will give a partial answer that must be weighed with the one source of information about faith, the Bible.

Warning: The path suggested here is not an easy one to take, because it means putting aside ways of thinking that are characteristic of our time. Ours is an age of science, or broadly speaking, of knowledge. Observing, gathering, analyzing, classifying, using knowledge—these make up the "language" of our time. To turn to the Bible is to turn to another language. This is, of course, literally true, because the Bible was written in ancient tongues and with literary forms and ways of thinking that are not current today. It may seem, therefore, anachronistic to turn to the language of the Bible, especially if we attempt to do so, for the moment, exclusively, putting aside the language of our time. Yet it may be true that the language of the Bible is as essential and as universal as the prevalent thought patterns of today.

As a practical step in preparation, try to put out of mind all definitions of faith. If you have thought about them or talked them over with others, they will be sufficiently in your conscious thoughts that you will be able to set them aside for the moment.

AN ANSWER

The Biblical picture of faith, put in the fewest possible words, is *God - man*. What the Bible tells about faith is the story of the meeting between God and man—one meeting in particular, but others as well. All these meetings, related to the past, show the man of faith how God meets man today.

In the story of faith, God meets specific (not statistically typical) men at particular times amid the imperfect details of their lives and situations. God does not prove his existence (although if moderns were rewriting the story, that is how they would have it begin), and then make pronouncements about his nature by which man can know him. He acts among men. The Ten Commandments, now commonly regarded as generalized rules of conduct, are the personal, direct teaching (words) of God to his people. The prophets do not speak systematically about God or about man, and then ask that people apply their teachings. They speak of the relationship existing between God and his people at that time, in that historical situation. Neither does Jesus Christ deal in generalities about God or about teachings to be stored up for future use. He confronts men with himself and thus with God, and is concerned with the responses of men at that moment.

Each of these clues to faith, coming from the "then," was once a "now." They inform the "now" of the learner today, the now of *God - man* that is faith. It is only in the Biblical story of faith that we learn of the relationship between God and man. No one, by looking within himself, can discover it or learn anything about it. Nor can he look at the development and experiences of others and learn anything about it. The relationship between God and the person is hidden from the person himself and from others. The only clues to it are given in the story of faith recorded in the Scriptures.

Clearly, this is a different kind of knowledge, different from the knowledges that are the currency of modern times. It has an immediacy, the immediacy of *God - man* in the past, that is somehow related to the immediacy of *God - man* in the present. "Knowing" might be a better, and more Biblical, word for it.

Think, meditate, do not discuss. Reread the section above and let this view of faith penetrate.

TEMPTATIONS

The understanding protests the immediacy of faith in the Biblical sense. It protests because its possessor rightly senses that the immediacy may involve him. Better to let the understanding take the brunt of it than the self. Thus begin the temptations to transform the Biblical view of faith into something else.

Temptation One will be to transform immediacy into a concept or general principle, of which the simplest would be, "God meets man." In such a form it becomes comprehensible, teachable.

Temptation Two will be to psychologize it, to find an explanation in human behavior. The currently popular psychologization goes, "Everyone searches for God, so men find him." An older one suggests that a spiritual part of man meets the spirit of God. To the question, "What is faith?" psychology of any kind can speak only of man and man's ideas of God, but not of God.

Temptation Three will be to theologize, that is, to find a niche in a system of knowledge into which the fact of *God - man* will fit in a logical way. The result is like that of Temptation One, except that the concept will require more complex reasoning ability. Theology, because it starts with God, has something to say about both God and man. Its answer to the question, "What is faith?" is less one-sided than psychology's answer must be. But its answer is also knowledge.

Other temptations to transform the Biblical picture of faith will arise because common definitions make it easier to comprehend and to teach. *The* faith, a body of knowledge, is easier to teach. So is a set of attitudes, or a series of indefinable experiences, or an array of eternal principles, or the steps of natural growth.

What can be learned of faith in the Bible is not so understandable as its common definitions would suggest or so orderly as the descriptions of it made by the recognized fields of knowledge today. It is not so full of eternal verities and general principles as modern ways of thinking would like to make it appear. It must remain this difficult, un-principled thing—*God - man*.

The proper study of men of faith, to paraphrase an old saying, is neither God nor man, but *God - man*. Such study will base its educational approach on the fact that the record of *God - man* is a story. In an age much given to self-examination, to statistical analysis, and to factual knowledge, this clear and somewhat exclusive path is difficult to take. For church teachers, it is made more difficult by the fact that Christian education theory for many years has looked elsewhere for its foundations. The foundations offered by psychology, theology, and education, alone or together, although seemingly solid, do not take account of the only available information about faith.

Try comparing the Biblical picture of faith with all the other views of faith that you can think of. What temptations do you have to reduce the immediacy of faith by making it over into something understandable? If psychology, theology, and education cannot provide the bases for Christian education, what part should they play in teaching?

The Foundation for Study

Faith is the hidden relationship between God and man (which means between God and that junior high right there). It is specific (having to do with the largely unknown details of that young person's life and the time in which he lives) and immediate (here and now, not something to be reaped in the future after careful planting today). What can be known about faith is known only in the story of faith recorded in the Bible.

Study brings together the story of faith, in which the clues to this relationship are found, and the life story of the young adolescent, which is his inner life.

You have taken a second step in considering the nature of study concerned with the source of information about faith. Review Chapter 1 and experiment in your own mind with bringing together the inner life of the young person and the source of information about faith. How would this central purpose and process change your ideas of teaching?

3. What's the Difference?

The Teacher Looks at Aims

ON TARGET

Mrs. Aker's ball-point pen lightly skims over the lesson plan, comes to rest momentarily, underlines twice: "The purpose of the lesson is . . ."

Mr. Barber, reading an article in the parent–teacher magazine, pauses to think about a statement: "The aim of Christian education is . . ."

At the weekly planning meeting for the junior high department Miss Campbell opens the discussion by saying, "Our purpose this Sunday is . . ."

Think of some ways these statements might be completed. Find examples of purposes for individual lessons. Look back to the theories of Christian education in Chapter 2 and decide in each case what aim for Christian education is implied or stated.

How important to you are statements of purpose? In what ways do you make use of them?

"To help the pupils see that . . . ," or "To help junior highs understand . . ." are typical statements of purpose. They suggest outcomes in knowledge or understanding on the part of the pupils.

"To produce people with Christian character," "To guide growing Christians," "To produce Christians who think theologically," are some aims taken from the theories in Chapter 2. These aims suggest outcomes in kinds of persons the pupils are to become.

Most statements of purpose and aim can be divided between these two general types. All of them look for some outcomes in the pupils. The teacher's problem in planning his work is how to achieve such outcomes. Whatever else statements of purpose may be, they are assurances that, as a result of the teacher's and the pupils' work, the pupils are going to get somewhere.

The average Christian can demonstrate in his own experience that church teaching did get him somewhere. He may be able to show that he acquired pieces of knowledge that add up to a meaningful accumulation. He will have less difficulty showing that he has mastered moral principles and skills that he uses in daily life. The average teacher might well be lost if he could not be sure his work had demonstrable results like these.

But at the heart of Christian faith is not knowledge or knowing about or perfection, but knowing and being known, the immediacy of *God - man* now. Knowing–being known is the confrontation of the person by God over and over again. In that immediacy, the average Christian's accumulation of knowledge, great or small, is nothing. The very highest that he knows may be called into question. However, he can put his knowledge to use—as a barrier between him and any hearing of the word of God. For example, he can make his knowledge of God a substitute for God himself. Between God and man, the average Christian's character and goodness, no matter how well-developed, have no standing. The very best that he is may be nothing, except, again, a thing behind which he can hide from God (as in the story of Luther's life). Yet most teachers aim to produce pupils who have something and are something.

The radical difference in study, compared with other approaches in Christian education, is that it seems aimless. Learning in the Christian faith is different from other kinds of learning because, seemingly, it gets nowhere.

But—you have to have a purpose, or a sense of direction, or something to aim for!

But—if all my work isn't going to make a difference in the lives of the pupils, why bother?

But—I might as well resign now!

But—_____

(This space left for your personal protest.)

A PARALLEL

The "nowhere" that study gets to, if different from knowledge or skills, is nevertheless not vague. The knowing–being known of faith has its closest, though inexact, parallel in human relationships. How does anyone come to know a person close to him—the one he loves and whose life he has chosen to share, or one of his children?

John gets acquainted with Mary and wants to know her better. Does he come to know Mary through lessons that are subdivisions of a science of her? The question is absurd. Any man can testify that there is no such thing as a science of women and he would not want to study it if there were. The lover who sets out to know his beloved by reading a book of psychology is, in the commonsense view, a fool. And common sense is right.

Mary quietly observes John, recalling this occasion and that on which he gave way to her. She adds these bits of learning together and forms an idea of John. He is submissive, dependent on her, she feels. Then suddenly John acts quite otherwise. He exhibits his independence (after they are married, of course). If Mary is not blinded by her own image of John, she will wisely toss it out. John, the man is not bounded by her ideas of him.

As a mother, Mary learns how to handle John, Jr. She knows how to meet his two-year-old demands, when to give way to temper, when to deflect it. At four, John, Jr., is different and Mary has to make changes in her ways with him. The changes are small compared to the ones that Mary may need to make when John, Jr., is fourteen and she is confronted with an almost new person. A wise

Mary will, indeed, learn that there are no ways to "handle" her son, that he is John, Jr., a person who is not totally determined by her ideas of what he should be.

John or Mary or anyone else can approach another person, no matter how close to him, with predetermined concepts and methods of handling. Perhaps John's views are still those of a child. To him other people always take on the roles of the chief persons in the world of his childhood, his mother and father. Maybe Mary will always prefer to pigeonhole people so that she knows beforehand what to expect from them. Perhaps as parents, both John and Mary will find it easier to perfect ways to "handle" their children.

Yet John and Mary and their children will all feel that these ways are escapes, means of protection against one another. All of them, even if they seldom or never achieve it, will uneasily acknowledge that knowing is possible and is what each desires. Never will the hope or possibility of such knowing die within them.

Knower and known, each has a certain, often painful, openness to the other, who demands that self come out of itself and interact with another self. Each will cast about for barriers to set up against the other, in order to save the self. Yet the other person forces the knower to acknowledge him, to take account of him, to set aside the barriers and react to him; in other words, to live with him.

Judged by the standards of accomplishment in other areas of learning, where does this knowing of another person get the learner? Nowhere, except more deeply involved with another, and more open to the moments of insecurity when the self is truly confronted by him.

It is similar, though not exactly so, with learning in the Christian faith. The learner gets nowhere except more deeply in faith, that is, in the *God - man* relationship, and open yet again to the insecurity of being confronted by God, against whom he always puts up barriers. There is no growing sequence or terminal point in faith; the learner starts over time and again. He comes to know, but he does not accomplish. And all along he is known, in a way not true in human relationships. For God confronts man and calls him to respond. No man chooses God in the way that he chooses a mate, or creates God out of his own ideas as he creates children out of his own substance.

Reread the section "An Answer," in Chapter 2, then reread the section above. Try to describe in your own words what is said about faith. You may find it easier to describe what faith is not, by contrasting it with the usual views of faith.

In what ways would you say the relationship between God and man is different from that between human beings? In what ways is it similar?

On the basis of what has been said here, would it be appropriate to say that the aim of Christian education is knowing God? Why or why not?

A FOOTNOTE

The language of knowing or of faith is the elementary language of humanity. Thus, "forces the knower . . . to live with him," might just as well read, "forces the knower . . . to be a human being." Yet this language has a strangeness.

Compared with other kinds of knowledge, knowing is not highly regarded at the present time because it is not useful. The hallmark of valuable knowledge today is the fact that it can be applied. Science can be applied to more efficient production, more and better products, a rising standard of living. Depth psychology can be used to ensure that the lures for prospective buyers will work. Sociology can be applied in social planning, education, Girl Scouts, and community life.

The "useful knowledge" game goes on at a grass-roots level too. Who knows his neighbor except as a guide to the right thing to buy, do, and think? Why the overflowing supply of advice on how to handle husband, children, self, based on the application of sound psychological principles? Against such an array of useful knowledge, knowing comes off a second best. As soon as it becomes useful, it ceases to be itself and becomes knowledge. Indeed, it can be described only in an oblique way, more literary than scientific, more story than systematic knowledge. Thus it is often considered sentimental, unreal, inexact.

THE FOUNDATION FOR STUDY

Christians say that the Bible is the word of God. The statement is one of the basic principles of Protestantism. By it, believers signify their conviction that in and through the Bible, God makes himself known to men. Or do they?

"Word" in modern terms—and in spite of various capital-W theological interpretations made of it when applied to the Bible—means an abstraction, several times removed from its originator, stored on a page in order to communicate something at some time or other to a reader. The communication, being abstract, is comprehensible and learnable. It would be easy to demonstrate that most Christians interpret the Bible as the "word" of God in this sense. The Bible is considered to be comprehensible and learnable; its words add up to knowledge that can be applied to life.

In the Bible, the meaning of "word" is different. The word of God is the power of God coming directly to his people. Its quality is immediate and not abstract. The Biblical habit of describing God in human terms, so that he "talks" with Abraham and Moses, for example, is a stumbling block to the modern mind. Yet such pictures represent the power of God rather exactly. So great is the power of "word" that it can be equated with the power of creation and with Jesus Christ, the incarnate God. The power becomes obscured when the word of God is regarded as something comprehensible and something to be learned, instead of that through which God speaks to his people.

The individual Christian and the community of which he is a part, the church, have to listen to God, over and over again, for their very life. Christians have an obligation to the Bible (and also to the sacraments) as the means by which God makes himself known. They are not free to use this means of grace or not, as they wish. They are not free to use it in a casual way, for example, by relying on what they already know in order to hear nothing more. They are obligated to continual involvement with the Scriptures (and to worship). The obligation here is largely a matter of simple humanity. When someone speaks to you, you listen, or you take a hundred different means of not listening. The point is that God does not speak to his people in any other way. Christians have the choice of listening or not listening; but they have no faith except as they hear and respond to God's word to them.

"Knowing the Bible" is a commonly accepted aim for Christian education. What other common purposes imply that the Bible is comprehensible and learnable? Think, for example, of what teachers and others in your church would say about the importance of the Bible in church teaching.

Think about or discuss the difference between:

The Bible as knowledge that can be applied to life.

The Bible as that through which God speaks to his people.

Do you agree or disagree with the statement, "They have no faith except as they hear and respond to God's word to them"? Give reasons for your answer.

Do you consider that the obligation of Christians to the Bible, as suggested here, is an abridgment of the freedom of the Christian? How does this view change commonly accepted ideas of what it means to be a member of the church?

Study proposes to take seriously the conviction that God speaks to his people and the responsibility to listen to him.

What study will attempt is to bring together the word and the person—not, be it noted, God and the person, for only God does that.

Study will be a repeated turning to the Scriptures to listen, hear, and respond to what God is saying to his people.

This is the third and definitive statement about study, the heart of the matter. Look back to the other two definitions, given at the ends of the previous chapters, to remind yourself of the steps you have taken toward this understanding.

Perhaps you will want to try explaining study to another person, preferably someone who has not read and discussed with you. If you are discussing with other teachers, allow time for each one to express what study seems to mean to him, or how he thinks study differs from teaching and learning.

AHA'S AND SOME FURTHER QUESTIONS

Certain students of human behavior label the reaction of a person to a new idea as the "Aha" reaction. Roughly translated, the label means, "Oh, I see! That means thus-and-so." Or, as it was in the old comic strips, a glowing light bulb appears above the thinker's head.

Contemplating the nature of study, one might "Aha" over the realization that the young adolescent himself is responsible for his own study. He is or shortly will become a communicant member of the church, thus undertaking an obligation to the Scriptures as the means by which God speaks to him. No one can study for him and pass the results on to him. He must himself hear and respond to God's word. Study cannot be a task superimposed on him from the outside because it will be good for him or because the church has a tradition or a body of knowledge to give him. Study is an integral part of his life as a member of the church.

A sigh may well follow this "Aha." How can such an interpretation of church membership be made in the church as the junior highs experience it? The present nature of Christian education, with its emphasis on teaching–learning, teacher–pupil, eats away at the young person's responsibility. What the junior high will learn from observing the adult church is that, beyond a certain point, no one concerns himself further with the Bible, that almost no one undertakes study as a lifelong responsibility. Most of the Christians he observes are content to apply what they learned up to that certain point, or to let their minister study for them. How, then, can the young adolescent's obligation to study be made an integral part of his life as a member of the church?

A second "Aha" or a disconcerted "H'm-m" can be uttered at the understanding that the teacher is also one who has an obligation to study, and not merely so that he can teach. He has a lifelong responsibility of his own for listening to God's word. He stands alongside the young person as one who also starts over again and again. He studies for himself; he also studies with the junior high.

Many a teacher will sigh with relief at the realization that he has been let off the hook. Clearly he does not need to know so much more than the pupils. He is not the teacher who possesses something valuable enough to pass on to young people. Nor is he the shining example who will inspire youth to goodness. He is not the taskmaster who knows what junior highs should do and must motivate them to do it. The work that adult and young adolescent undertake is a responsibility they have in common. The entire structure of the teacher–pupil relationship has to be reconsidered in the light of that mutual responsibility for study. Most of the commonly accepted methods of teaching must also be rethought.

The adult and the young adolescent study within the context of the community, the church, in its present life. This "Aha" is the one that should give the basic shape to a program for young adolescents of which study is a part. It also means that the essential attitude of the church, and of adult and youth members, is one of hearing. At the same time the church makes possible the hearing. The only valid reason for the church's concern with Christian education is the fulfillment of its obligation to proclaim or to make possible the hearing of the word. The valid basis on which it can ask adults to work with young adolescents is that of helping to fulfill the obligation of the community as a whole.

Groans resound at this point. How will it be possible to let slip into limbo the rich promises that Christian education now makes, in favor of such a singularly oriented approach?

But, "Aha," and perhaps, "Alas," study cannot result in outcomes, as Christian education now promises to do. Study cannot result in knowledge or in skills, except at the risk of concentrating on the stumbling blocks to faith and bypassing the heart of the matter. Study can only look toward the kind of knowing suggested in the example of close human relationships. The outcome is God's alone; about it Christians have only a few clues in the story of faith. Study has no way to judge whether such knowing takes place, nor has it any right to know. It relies only on the promise that God makes himself known to his people. Study will have no way of measuring development or of knowing whether it has a successful outcome.

Thus, a loud and final "Aha," the proper statement of purpose or aim for Christian education can be formulated only on the basis of the responsibility of Christians— church, adult, and young adolescent—to involve themselves with the word of God. The sole function of church and teacher is to handle aright the word of God to his people and to make possible some hearing of it.

The "Aha's" or insights listed here are only some of the ones that might occur as a result of thoughtful consideration. What others occur to you?

Think about or discuss with others the implications suggested here. Some specifics are:

"How can the young adolescent's obligation to study be made an integral part of his life as a member of the church?" Especially in the light of the fact that most members of the church do not recognize any such obligation.

"The entire structure of the teacher–pupil relationship has to be reconsidered in the light of that mutual responsibility for study." What changes might be necessary in approach to teaching, class structure, methods?

"Most of the commonly accepted methods of teaching must also be rethought." See the next chapter, which you may want to study before discussing the problem.

For more on "the basic shape of program . . . of which study is a part," see *The Young Adolescent in the Church* (The Geneva Press, 1962).

Contrast the approaches to Christian education that promise outcomes with the responsibility-oriented approach of study. How do you feel about an approach to teaching that can hold no promise of outcomes or ways of measuring development?

Try formulating in your own words, or as the result of group discussion, a valid statement of aim for the Christian education of young adolescents.

If study so far seems aimless and unprincipled, it has, nevertheless, form, some expectations of what it can do, and some clues as to how to proceed. These are the concerns of Chapter 4.

4. How to Get Nowhere

The Teacher Looks
at Methods

"Well, in *our* country," said Alice, still panting a little [after a run with the Red Queen that ended under the same tree they had started from], "you'd generally get to somewhere else—if you ran very fast for a long time as we've been doing."

"A slow sort of country!" said the Queen. "Now, *here,* you see, it takes all the running *you* can do, to keep in the same place. If you want to get somewhere else, you must run at least twice as fast as that!"

Let this quotation from *Through the Looking-Glass* warn anyone who has eased back, saying to himself, "Well, if I don't have to know so much more than the pupils, and we aren't going to get anywhere anyhow . . ." It may be that the methods appropriate to study will make the teacher do all the running he can or run twice as fast.

It is a more or less true insight that the teacher is relieved of having to know so much. In study the adult is not the dispenser on the bottle of knowledge. Teacher and pupils are not primarily face-to-face with each other but are essentially face-to-face with the Scripture. The teacher's function is to help the young adolescent undertake the responsibility for study that falls on him as one who is or shortly will become a communicant member of the church. The adult, standing alongside the young person, is a guide in exploration of the story of *God - man.* He has no other aim than to make possible some hearing of the word of God.

Is Study This?

With such an apparently simple aim in mind, the teacher might:

—train young adolescents in the habit of devotional or inspirational reading of a verse or several verses of the Bible each day (considered a valuable outcome of Christian education).

—demonstrate to the pupils how to find guidance by opening the Bible to any verse (rare, but not unknown; many teaching methods are based on the assumption that such would be possible).

—select a passage of the Bible and weave around it all the thoughts, quotations, life experiences, and bits of poetry that relate to it (as in many a sermon and lesson lecture).

—start with a problem or need of young people and search the Bible passage for an answer to it (always surprisingly easy to find).

—use a Bible passage to show the junior highs how to be good (by locating a moral principle they can apply to life).

—help young people get acquainted with Bible material as a good thing to know and part of their cultural background (so that when someone gives them a test of Bible knowledge they can choose one of three answers showing that they know who Jehoshaphat was).

Using the Old Testament story of Joseph, it is easy to construct the forms of these kinds of involvement with Scripture, which are, by and large, the ones that young adolescents now learn.

Before reading farther, review the story of Joseph in Gen., chs. 37; 39:1 to 46:7.

The junior high who sets out to read the lengthy story of Joseph by the devotional method of a verse or verses a day will take about a year to complete the task and will then have no idea what the story is about. What would he find for guidance in, for example, Gen. 37:12: "Now his brothers went to pasture their father's flock near Shechem"? No teacher would advise such a procedure; he would choose other, more "devotional" parts of the Bible to recommend. Yet many teachers proceed in classwork in a verse-by-verse method, stopping at each number for drill or a brief lecture.

What will the wandering finger find if it turns to the story of Joseph to locate a guiding verse for the day? (Try it.) The searcher will start over again many times or give up in despair. Or he will let the Bible fall open again where it is much more likely to fall open by itself, namely, among the psalms.

Both of these approaches—and perhaps they are only one—regard the Bible as useful knowledge lying about in golden nuggets of verse, available for a small amount of digging. The method tears most parts of the Bible into little pieces, except for those which are already in pieces, such as The Proverbs. Essentially, such an approach refuses to recognize that the books of the Bible were written as books, that is, with coherent sentences related to other sentences in paragraphs and in stories and episodes. Not only does it reduce the narrative nature of the Bible; it also reduces the historical nature of the story it tells.

The sermon or lesson lecture can be constructed easily on the basis of the story of Joseph. Suppose it started with the scene in which Joseph forgives his brothers. A search through the concordance will locate appropriate parts of Scripture that deal with forgiveness. A similar search through Bartlett's *Familiar Quotations* will yield bits of human wisdom about forgiveness, ranging from Shakespeare to Edgar Guest. Current books on successful living and the *Reader's Digest* will furnish true-life stories of how forgiveness pays. Presto, a lecture, based on the assumption that everyone knows the Bible story, that forgiveness is easy and human, as demonstrated by the wisdom of the ages, and that it can be readily commended to the hearers. The approach reduces the Bible to useful knowledge equivalent to human wisdom. (Not all sermons are of this type, of course, but the example will have a ring of familiarity to many churchgoers.)

Almost everyone has brothers or sisters, or at least lives in a family. Young adolescents have problems in getting along with others. Learning to do so is one of the developmental goals of their age group. The need offers a good starting point for considering the story of Joseph. To be sure, the teacher who takes such an approach must skip over or treat in a negative way the fact that the brothers did not get along. He will need to move quickly toward the positive lesson that, in the end, they lived happily together because Joseph became a good guy and forgave the others. God, incidentally, can be shown to have helped in the process. The story is reduced to the learnable principle that forgiving helps in getting along with others, and junior highs are supposed to apply the principle to their own actions.

The teacher who wants to help junior highs be good might take the problem-centered approach or he might hold up Joseph as an example to them. By skipping over much of the story, he can show that Joseph is one of the Heroes of the Ages, worthy of emulation. The Joseph who in the story is a fairly real person is reduced to a shining, cardboard image, unreal, unattractive, and easily forgotten along with other shining examples.

The "knowing the Bible" approach is one of the simplest. The teacher need merely go over the story, trying to make it interesting, and then drill the young people on the various points and people in it. He can devise any number of simple tests to make sure the junior highs recognize Joseph, Pharaoh, famines, dreams, etc., and will recognize them forever and ever. Young people who are naturally endowed with good memories win hands down in such contests of Biblical literacy.

Study is different from any of these common types of involvement with Scripture. It has its own characteristic methods derived from the unknowable nature of the story of faith, from the unlearnable nature of faith, and from the unobservable nature of the inner life of young adolescents.

Do you agree that the kinds of involvement with Scripture listed and illustrated here are the ones that young people are, by and large, now learning? Can you give other examples of them?

Decide what view of the Bible underlies each approach. List them. With which do you most nearly agree? With which do you disagree? Why? If you are working with a group of teachers, discuss these views in the light of what you think the Bible is. Again, you will find many different opinions. Keep in mind the distinction made in Chapter 3 between something comprehensible and learnable, and that through which God speaks to his people.

THE BASIC METHOD: LIVING INTO

The general method of the work shared by adult and young adolescents is "living into," or identification. The purpose is to bring together the story of faith and the inner life of the young person for the illumination of his hidden life with God. The story of faith in the Bible can also be described as the drama of *God - man*. It is also the history of faith, the events of which can, for the most part, be located in time and place.

Identification with this story-drama-history is similar to what happens when a person reads a story or sees a play. He "lives into" the persons and actions, becoming identified with the characters, perceiving their dilemmas, and for the moment, taking them on as his own. When he finishes the story or leaves the theater or turns away from the TV, he may not be able to systematize or describe what he has learned but he has been moved and given new insights that sometime later he may be able to perceive and express consciously.

Almost everyone is familiar with "living into" as it is described here. Think of occasions on which you have lived into a story or play. How much do you value what you gained on such occasions? Which did your experience resemble more: "learning" in the usual sense, or "knowing" as developed in Chapter 3?

The following guidelines to study are all concerned with the use of Bible material. The order in which they are given is not necessarily the order in which any session of study would proceed. Detailed methods based on these guidelines are described in Chapters 6 through 10.

A STORY IS A STORY

Study seeks to develop the story in the Bible material fully, letting it go where it goes, letting it say what it says, so that identification is possible. ("Story," as used here, does not mean fiction.)

Suppose the teacher is preparing to tell the story of Joseph. He may make an outline of the story as a guide to learning it. What happens if he reads his outline to the class instead of telling the story? He then tells only the skeleton of the story. It lacks flesh and blood; it lacks people and their feelings and actions and the things that happen to them. Or suppose the storyteller decides to abbreviate several passages of conversation in the story and to tell in a general way what happened. In doing so he omits important details of interaction among persons in the story. The good storyteller does not generalize or abbreviate but tries to recite every detail of the narrative. The details are the raw material of identification.

Especially in the case of a long, complicated story like that of Joseph, it is tempting to look for an extractable "theme." One theme of the story is that God provides for his people, or, as expressed in a theological category, providence. What would happen if the teacher announced the theme beforehand and then set about to find it in the story, depriving the narrative of its suspense and climax? The result would be boredom. Yet this seemingly farfetched example is equivalent to telling the pupils at the beginning of the class or the teacher at the head of his printed materials, "The purpose of this lesson is . . ."

Suppose the teacher proceeds the other way, by engaging the class in becoming acquainted with the story, including the details of Joseph's dreams, the gift of the coat from his father, Reuben's dissent with the plot of his brothers, the repetitious tests Joseph made of his brothers, and all the other details. At some point or other, almost every junior high can live into the story. He too is jealous, thinks himself superior, wishes his father loved him more, wants to kill, does not dare trust those who have once hurt him.

These are some of the points of identification. They need not be labeled or especially pointed out; the story itself presents them to the conscious and unconscious levels of understanding. Such points of identification are not present for the young adolescent if the narrative is killed by taking shortcuts, by rushing the story along to a theme within it, or by twisting it to fit a theme not found in it at all.

The points of identification are not the "problems" the pupil brings to the Bible to which he is going to find some solutions. Neither are they the "sins" of which the pupil is to be convicted and from which he must be saved. They are the characteristic actions of men, the men with whom God has dealings. According to the direction set for study, there is no reason for the young person to learn or to be drilled in the details of a story. It should be of no concern to the teacher whether the pupil knows or recognizes the story of Joseph two years hence or ever again.

Provided the classwork has been true to the story, it should be possible to leave with the young adolescent the impact of the drama without much interpretation. Let it speak to him what it will on whatever level and at whatever time he needs or can absorb it. The distinctive power of the story lies in the fact that its narrative interest speaks to and engages the hearer at many different levels that are unknowable to the outsider (i.e., the teacher) and somewhat unknowable to the hearer himself. In contrast, a theme or principle drawn from the story speaks chiefly to the intellect. Unknown and unpredictable learnings are usually called incidental learnings—at least, they seem incidental to teachers and curriculum planners, who tend to cling to one definable purpose. They may be less incidental than they are commonly thought to be; perhaps they get closer to the heart of the matter where faith is concerned.

The story of faith is more than the easily identified stories in the Bible, such as that of Joseph. The Bible stories were long considered the appropriate teaching material for children. Therefore, it is supposed, everyone has absorbed them early and still remembers them. This popular myth blinds many teachers to the fact that the Bible tells a longer, continued story into which fit the stories and the history and most of the other literature. The story begins with Abraham, with a prelude in prehistory, and ends, as far as the Bible is concerned, with the founding and early years of the church and some indications about the end of history.

Just as it is possible to distort an individual story by reducing it to a theme or twisting it to fit a theme, so it is possible to distort the total story. Teachers who are overanxious to have junior highs learn Bible history reduce the story of faith to the dullest kind of history, made up not of people and God but of dates, events, eras. Certain curriculum materials, chiefly nondenominational ones, delight in trotting out charts of eras and millennia, often mysteriously arrived at and bearing little relation to the story of faith.

Some parts of the Bible do not seem to be story or history. What of the books of the prophets, for example? At first glance they seem to be teachings that can be detached from the story of faith. A common way of teaching such materials is to present the prophets as heroes of the faith. Yet in both the books of the prophets and in the corresponding narrative material in other Old Testament books, there continues the story of the people of God to whom the prophets spoke. Identification will thus be made with the people of the prophets' times who heard their teachings as the words of God. The New Testament letters can be read as detached teachings or theology until it is seen that they were written as actual letters to actual situations in the churches. Behind them are the persons who wrote them and the persons to whom they were addressed. They too are a part of the story of the people of God. The psalms are commentaries on the story of faith, often retelling it. Other types of books are also commentaries on the central story of Scripture; still others have only an indirect relationship to it.

Problems will arise in following the guidelines of letting the story speak for itself. One of them is the sheer length of some stories, such as that of Joseph. Another occurs because of the structure of some Old Testament books. For example, accounts of the crossing of the Red Sea, given in Exodus, are made up of several versions of the story woven together in such a way as to preserve all of them. One verse gives one version of the event; the next gives another version, not supplementary to the first, but contradictory to it. Most teachers do not have enough knowledge of the Bible to trace one version or to put different ones together into a story. Because of these two problems and some others, the teacher must often rely on printed materials to make for him the necessary selection of verses.

The method of developing a story with thoroughness and fidelity need not be storytelling, and, in most cases, should not be. Young adolescents should work with the Bible itself. There are numerous way in which they can be helped to find and develop the fullness of a story on their own. Many teaching suggestions made in curriculum materials are intended to aid this process. Usually, however, teachers consider them to be ways of "making it more interesting" for the pupils.

If you have previously listed different views of the Bible, you should now be able to compare them with the Bible seen as the story of faith. Some of these views are widely popular and traditional in the church's teaching program. In what ways do they make it difficult to understand the Bible as a continued story of the people of God? For example, the golden-nuggets, or verse-by-verse, view? the moral guidance view? the solving-our-problems view?

In curriculum materials the methods suggested for full development of a story and for identification are often more complex than they might seem from the general description above. What has been given here is the underlying reason for them. Look through some teaching plans that take up Bible material. See if you can spot suggested steps or techniques directed toward full development of the story and toward identification.

Try transferring what has been said here about an Old Testament story to a story from the New Testament, for example, the account of Jesus' preaching at Nazareth. As source material, use Luke 4:16–30. What if the story were given in outline form? What if the theme were announced and the pupils directed to find the proof of it in the story? What if the story were told fully or the pupils guided in exploring it fully? A warning: at first you will tend to develop the story in terms of Jesus Christ alone because it is customary to approach the Gospels as sources of *information about* Jesus. Rethink your approach in light of the understanding that the Gospels are part of the story of *God - man*. With whom will the junior highs identify?

SEEING INTO

In addition to "incidental" learnings of identification, *study will look specifically for identification with the God - man situation in Bible material.*

"Insight," or "seeing into," is a good word for this, meaning a realization that goes beyond previous understanding, and is not so much the result of thought as the beginning of thought. Insight results from the dramatic, that is, the "living into," impact of the story. It is often surprising, and different from commonly accepted ideas; it tends to make the hearer pause. For example, in the story of Joseph, God does not merely provide for his people in spite of the ill-intentioned acts of men; he provides for his people through them. Such a way of dealing with men makes no sense from the commonsense, human point of view. Catching a glimpse of God at work in such a way calls the learner up short.

The resulting pause for thought requires development in the class session, unlike the result of incidental learnings, an area in which the teacher keeps hands off. Most frequently the development is carried out in discussion. The teacher does not need to point out or belabor the moral of the story—in human terms it is seldom "moral." He does not need to tie it all up with a sermon or lesson to drive home an understanding. His function, rather, is to help the pupils express what they feel and think about the story and to generate a thoughtful consideration that may extend beyond classwork. Thoughtfulness, and not a logical conclusion, is the aim in the development of insight.

In response to the story of Joseph, some junior highs, judging by common moral standards, may be struck by the thought that all the people in the story seem unworthy of any notice from God. None of them are very commendable types. Some pupils may have sensed the wonder of God's way of working but reject the insight. It is too much out of accord with what they would have expected. Others may silently wonder about the insight. Still others may provisionally accept it but wish to compare it with other ideas.

The teacher's work is to bring out such reactions to insights from the story. Young adolescents seldom miss the central meaning of a story in terms of faith, provided they have freedom to think and are encouraged always to question their own ideas and those which others have taught them. Usually some of the comments of the young people will show an awareness of the meaning if the classwork has faithfully developed the story. There are ways in which the teacher can, if necessary, help the pupils grasp the meaning without launching into a sermon or a lesson.

The central meaning or insight of the story is not a piece of learning to be memorized or even accepted. It is a beginning place for thinking, considering, weighing. The young people may reject it, accept it, store it away for later thought, argue it, welcome it, dislike it, think it impossible, feel uncomfortable in the face of it, and so on, through numerous possible reactions. There is no conformity in faith.

What would you say is the difference between an insight from a story and the theme of a story?

The methods used for this aspect of study are varied. Look at some teaching plans and see if you identify methods directed toward locating and developing the impact of a story in terms of faith.

Remember that this chapter takes up the general approach to study and the reasons behind the methods it uses. Specific methods and how to use them are described in Chapters 6 through 10.

How would you feel about class discussion with young adolescents that aimed at thoughtfulness and not at reaching a conclusion? Impatient? Challenged? Discouraged? Hopeful? As though you had not accomplished anything? Satisfied? Frustrated? Stirred to do some thinking of your own? In other words, how much are you able to think along with young adolescents?

UNBUILDING

Study recognizes the necessity for breaking down some concepts already present in the pupil's mind so that there may be a hearing of the word of God.

"To question their own ideas and those which others have taught them." The surprise of insight and the unsettling nature of faith as the meeting between God and man make it necessary for the teacher to keep this possibility open to young adolescents.

There are three myths in current Christian education that make it difficult to admit such a necessity. One is the theory of teaching faith step by step. Closely related is the extreme care taken, at least in theory, to avoid teaching little children anything that might have to be unlearned later. The third is the idea that Christian teaching is essentially of a piece with all other learning. Added to these is the popular belief that a teacher need only accentuate the positive to achieve some golden, unbroken thread of learning. For example, in the opinion of many one need only teach Americanism and capitalism in a positive way and ignore the existence of communism to produce good Americans.

Most teachers can show from their own observations that young adolescents have learned many things, both inside and outside the church, that have to be unlearned because they stand in the way of perceiving anything about faith. As an example from depth, the word "sin," so frequently and carelessly thrown at young people, means to many of them (and to many adults) certain forbidden sexual thoughts and practices in which they may have indulged.

Many junior highs hold the concept that faith is the struggle of the conscience to be good. By extension, the death of Jesus Christ makes up for the failure of the individual conscience. Such a concept has usually been planted by church school teachers.

Often teachers find that junior highs have a closed-circuit view of the story the Bible tells. If asked to consider why there is evil in the world, some young people will come up with the answer, "There had to be or Jesus Christ would not have come." Such dead-end reasoning is also the result of previous teaching in the church.

From many outside sources, especially their schools, young people have come to understand faith as religion, "worshiping the god of your choice." They have some difficulty with the insight that God chooses his own people because such a view is undemocratic compared to the safe, general view of religion.

Such examples could be multiplied and would include some parental views and teachings. They show that before the way is open for hearing the story of faith, there are some formidable barriers to expose, reconsider, and break down.

Everyone sets up barriers against the hearing of the

word of God. It would be unrealistic not to expect to find some among the things that young people have been taught. However, teachers of young adolescents are not hereby invited to a gripe session against the former teachers of their pupils. No amount of careful planning can in the long run avoid the barriers of misunderstanding and of too simple understanding. (What junior high teachers themselves do is another matter to be taken up in another section.)

There is no way in which that which the church teaches is continuous with other learnings of any kind. The church has to claim and act in its difference. The wise adult who works with junior highs usually finds that he must dissociate himself from the views and values of their parents. He does so not in order to consolidate himself with the young people by putting himself on their side of a struggle. He does so because he wants young adolescents to be free to question any concepts that faith may force them to question. He wants them to be able to hear the word of God and to be thoughtful.

The popular way of "accentuating the positive" omits the process of thoughtfulness, of reconsideration, of self-criticism, that is necessary in faith. It is the way of indoctrination.

In study with young adolescents, unlearning often begins with sharp confrontation. The story, if allowed to speak for itself, will have an impact that cuts across the pupils' understandings. Insights from the story of Joseph challenge sensible ideas of how God works among men. Clearly they also challenge some ideas about God that young people have been taught previously. Perhaps also they cut across the ways men willfully prefer to think of God.

Few young people are comfortable when their own or commonly held ideas are challenged, especially in the church. Often they will conceal what they have perceived because they think the teacher will not tolerate their saying it aloud. The insight they have gained might seem revolutionary. The fact may be satisfying to them inwardly but they learned long ago that discretion in the face of authority and tradition is the better part of valor. The teacher, therefore, must take the initiative in making it possible for junior highs to express themselves and in sharpening the contrast between the insights of faith and the usual ideas.

Sometimes both teacher and pupils recall and identify different points of view, usually labeled as someone else's to prevent the young people from having to be immediately self-critical. What the teacher is *not* doing in this stage of the work is saying to the young person: "Your ideas are wrong! I will show you a better idea . . ."; or, "What the church believes and you must believe is . . ." Rather, the teacher is making opportunity for the young person to look at his own views. The more these are brought to the level of thought and verbal expression, the more it is possible to weigh them against other possibilities.

To sum up the first three guidelines, study seeks identification on many different levels of feeling and thought, most of which are not observable or knowable to either teacher or young adolescent. Beyond this, study seeks to appeal to the thinking, considering, and weighing processes by which the young person balances for a time in his understanding a new insight, comparing it with others. The outcome, even in terms of the pupil's eventual understanding, is beyond the responsibility of the teacher.

Do not underestimate the popularity of "accentuating the positive" today. Some people say that indoctrination is all right provided the thing children are to be indoctrinated with is good. Call to mind several members of your church and imagine yourself explaining to them that junior highs should be free to examine and question anything, even the church. How would they react?

Can you think of other examples of concepts young people hold that can be barriers to hearing the word of God?

Why are thoughtfulness, reconsideration, and self-criticism necessary in faith?

Look through your teaching materials for methods directed toward challenging or breaking down previously learned ideas.

For a real hoedown of a discussion in a group of teachers, try this question: What is your opinion of an approach to Christian education that includes unlearning but not learning?

TIME AND PLACE

Study includes the fullest possible development of the factual and historical background of Bible material.

Many junior highs (and some adults) believe that all Bible stories are fanciful, or that events took place somewhere out there "in heaven," or that they never took place at all. For the most part, junior highs have been taught that what matter are the abstract "lessons" to be drawn from the Scriptures.

Yet the story of faith, by and large, is the story of real happenings and persons. Events took place at definable times amid historical situations, and involved real people. In this fact, especially in the coming of Jesus Christ in a time and place, lies the difference between faith and eternal truth into which faith is always being transformed.

The Ten Commandments offer one of the best examples of this kind of transformation. Today it is almost impossible to consider them in anything like their original meaning or importance. They have come to be regarded as universal laws, so universal that they well might offer the meeting point for all faiths. Surely, the thinking goes, Muslim, Buddhist, Moral Re-Armament, Christian, agnostic, humanist, and everyone else can agree that these moral standards are what all men strive for. Many Christians believe that the sum and substance of faith is keeping the commandments. Loyal and superloyal Americans recognize them as the basis of the American way of life. Curiously and significantly enough, it is often people who will have nothing to do with the church who most loudly uphold the cause of keeping the commandments.

What such universalizing does is to cut away the particularity and the peculiarity of the story of faith. It does away with the people whom God has chosen—such a peculiar thing for him to do; with the circumstances of their time—which might show how the laws were more particular and less general than is supposed; with the way the people regarded the laws—not as laws at all but as direct teaching from God; with God—or at least the God of Israel; with the total story of faith—since Jesus Christ and Paul might dash cold water on enthusiasm for keeping the commandments.

Some aspects of the story of faith are offensive; they just do rub people the wrong way. It is possible to get around them by universalizing the good and acceptable and ignoring the rest. (As another example, consider what has been done with Jesus Christ or with the Christmas story.) That is what the world always does with faith. It is what Christians do also when they extract a lesson and ignore the particular people, situations, history, and events through which God worked.

Some curriculum materials make a great deal of background facts in order to prove that the Bible is "true" and worthy of the young person's attention. This is not the point (and seems to stem from some original doubt anyway). The truth of the Bible story is in what God says through it to his people. But that word of God, both then and now, is spoken to the person in his time and place, not in some spiritual realm or in timelessness. Bible teaching that is driven to locate a timeless lesson leaves itself hanging out in the air where the young adolescent can easily ignore it. Or he is left with the idea that at some future time when he and everyone else is perfect and spiritual and the world is at peace, then it will all come true.

The point is, rather, that God speaks to his people today in this world. Because of and on behalf of this world—the world of wars and scientific advance and fear and hope and violence, in which we grope for the meaning of it all—he chooses his people and calls them to be his own. Only as young adolescents can see in some detail the worlds (that is, the times and places) of the people to whom God spoke in the past and the ways they were called to serve their worlds, can they come to see that God is concerned with them in their time and place.

The work of developing such details, fact-finding, is something that most young adolescents enjoy doing, and it can be made part of the session or part of work done outside class time. Often it requires the use of outside resources. As with the details of a story, background and historical details are not material for memorizing or drill. Bible geography and history can be the dullest of subjects when pursued for themselves. They serve rather the purpose of identification.

A few problems must be faced. One of them is that some parts of the Bible are nonhistorical material—the stories in Genesis preceding those about Abraham, for example. They are prehistorical, which does not mean that they tell about people who lived in caves and wore skins, but that they cannot be related to specific times and places. They existed long before written records were made. Perhaps some of them originated in actual happenings. As they were told and retold over the centuries, the historical kernels were lost and the stories became legendary. Others of these stories are more like myths, in that they explain certain observable facts about life, such as the fact that men rebel against God. They are true in the same sense that the entire Bible is true but they are not about actual happenings in the historical sense. If junior highs are inclined to take such stories literally, the teacher must press the question of their meaning in the context of the story of faith. Often the way to do so is semiliterary. That is, it includes finding out why such stories are included in the Bible, where they came from, what they meant to those who collected them and put them in final form.

Some stories that are historical contain fanciful and legendary details. For example, no one can accept The Book of Judges as a literal description of the conquest of Canaan in the face of evidence that events took place otherwise. Details were heightened and time foreshortened to emphasize the glory of God and what he did for his people. Some of the leaders were considerably enlarged and heroized. Details of this sort, rightly used within a story, usually carry their own meaning. They would do so more if Christians could loosen themselves from a literal and altogether serious approach to the Bible and see that parts of it are outrageous and humorous exaggerations.

Both these problems indicate a sub-guideline. Part of the factual and historical background necessary for Bible study includes information about the collecting and writing of the books themselves.

Go back through this section and select or mark those ideas which are new or striking to you (over which you may have exclaimed "Aha") and those which puzzle you most. If you are working with a group, discuss both kinds of statements.

What does it matter whether young adolescents believe that Bible stories are make-believe or not?

What is the difference between a universal truth deduced from Scripture and the here-and-nowness of faith as suggested here? Why does a timeless lesson result in something the young person can easily ignore?

Try to express in your own words the reason for the importance of developing the factual and historical background of Bible material.

Are the conditions of the world in which the young adolescent lives the "problems" he will bring to the Bible? Why or why not?

As you see it, what happens to young people when they are forced to believe that Adam and Eve were real persons? What happens to the story when such a literal interpretation is made?

A LARGER VIEW

In study the adult bears a greater responsibility to the Scripture than the young adolescent.

At one point, the teacher, although still one who studies with the pupils, is in no sense equal to them. The adult bears the responsibility for a framework of understanding beyond that of the pupils. The way in which the adult perceives the material to be studied is, by and large, the way in which it will be approached in classwork. He is not a vacuum any more than the young adolescent is. He too brings to study his own ideas, including some that have to be unlearned. What appears in the young person as something to be unlearned in the work of study can become in the adult a barrier to any study at all because he is the guide in study. The crucial question to be faced is: Will the adult's understanding prevent or make possible any hearing of the word of God?

No story, episode, or event in the story of faith can be approached by itself but must be seen in the light of the continued story that the Bible tells. This is a working principle of the larger framework that the adult must have. How will it affect what the teacher does with the story of Joseph?

One meaning of this episode in the story of faith lies in the fact that God worked for the good of his people in and through the evil actions of men. The story is about the family whom God had chosen and whose descendants became the people of God. The episode takes place, therefore, within the context of the history of God's people, which culminates in Jesus Christ and the forming of a new people. One meaning of the crucifixion is similar to what the Joseph story shows about God's ways of working. God did not wait for men to be so good as to refrain from destroying his Son but worked in and through the ill-intentioned acts of men. The meaning of the one story has a continuity with the total story. The entire story of faith, but especially its central acts in the meeting of God and man in Jesus Christ, is the larger framework of understanding for any episode in it.

Viewed outside of its context and taken in isolation, the story of Joseph takes on different meanings. A common view of it, found in Bible storybooks for children and in some church school lessons, is that Joseph was a good guy and that young people should be like him. Suppose a teacher, being only half prepared, takes such a view of the story. It becomes a lesson in moralism or hero worship, wrenching the story out of shape and out of its place in the story of faith. Perhaps the teacher regards the story as a lesson in successful living—brothers get along better if someone, like Joseph, forgives. The possible interpretations are numerous. These two have the noticeable defect of leaving God out of account except, perhaps, as an upholder of the good guy or a promoter of forgiveness, that is, as one who does what human beings want him to do.

It may be worthwhile to consider for a moment the possible reactions of young people to such partial and rootless interpretations. If they get to look at the full story, some alert ones are going to see that Joseph wasn't a good guy. Probably they will keep such knowledge to themselves and quietly classify the teacher with a number of other deficiencies—especially in the matter of truthfulness—that they observe in the church. Most junior highs react with outright or concealed boredom at being told what to do or whom to admire. In both cases, missing the meaning of the story in faith, the teacher will also miss engaging the junior highs at a sufficiently deep level. No amount of preaching or interest getting will make up for the lack.

The teacher must work within a broader context than his own ideas. He too stands face-to-face with the Scripture, to be challenged and corrected by it. Insights from the story of faith will cut across his ideas many times, sometimes in the midst of the work with young adolescents. But some of the corrections had better take place before he meets with the class. Otherwise he may be concentrating on the barriers to faith and missing the heart of the matter.

This is not a counsel of perfection. No one understands perfectly; in the long run, no one comprehends. Anyone who thinks he does becomes a giver, not a guide. Neither is the adult required to adhere to and respresent a doctrine held by the church. But the adult is responsible for making possible some hearing of the word of God.

Here theology enters the picture of study at its proper place of responsibility, not as the subject matter to be taught, but as the informative, corrective discipline for the adult who works with young adolescents. One of the things that curriculum materials do for the teacher is to supply a framework of interpretation by recalling for him the total story of faith.

Look through your teaching material for points at which a framework of interpretation is given for the teacher.

The matter of using theology as a corrective discipline is trickier than it may seem from the brief discussion here. Chapter 5 takes up some of the benefits and dangers of being theologically responsible.

Why must the teacher's ideas be challenged and corrected? Is there one "line" to which he must adhere? Is it not true that Protestants are free to interpret the Bible for themselves? In what ways might the teacher's ideas lead to concentrating on the barriers to faith?

Resolved: Since everyone sets up barriers against hearing the word of God, it is foolish to be so concerned to avoid them. Debate the proposition.

The general methods outlined here are developed in more
detail in the following places:
Responsibility for own study—Chapter 7, "Planning"
Developing Bible material—Chapter 9, "Learning to Read"
Identification—Chapter 10, "Considering"; also Chapter 9
Unlearning—Chapter 10
Time and place—Chapter 8, "Fact-finding"; also Chapter 7
A larger view—Chapter 5, "The Breadth and Length
and Height and Depth"; Chapter 6, "Homework—the
Teacher's"

5. The Breadth and Length and Height and Depth

The Teacher Looks at Theology

THE MAKING OF A LAY THEOLOGIAN

"I don't know enough!" cries C.T., the Conscientious Teacher, who has been learning about study as a responsibility shared by teacher and adolescent in the church. "Great!" thought C.T. when he realized that, as the adult guide in study, he would not need to be so many jumps ahead of his pupils. At least, he did not need a superior store of knowledge to pass on to them. Then it began to appear that he would be required to know something after all, perhaps a great deal. It would seem that, as the adult guide in study, he was responsible for whether or not the word of God was handled rightly. How would he know the right way?

C.T. found help at hand, once he began to look for it. His curriculum materials provided interpretation for his own background study, but often the interpretation did not come to rest where he thought it would. Sometimes a new idea seemed to be just what he had always thought but had never been able to express. Other times he grumbled that someone was tampering with long-established and perfectly all right beliefs. He found to his surprise that different interpretations of the same material could be and were made in his background reading. Which was he supposed to follow?

Looking for more authoritative guidance, C. T. went to the church library and borrowed some books on theology. And what did he find? There are many theologies. Theology is full of controversies. It is a difficult (he felt at times) and a challenging (he felt at other times) subject. C.T. was made to think, but he became more confused.

His patience ran thin in the search for truth. Finally he cornered his minister and demanded, "What *does* the church believe?" In other words, C.T. wanted to know the line he was supposed to teach. He nearly gave up being one who studies and who guides young adolescents in study. But who could blame him?

How familiar is C.T.'s experience to you? Have you ever delved into theology only to become more confused than you were before?

Suppose C.T. has voiced his question about what the church believes at a teachers meeting. What would you say in answer to him? What sources of help would you suggest to him?

THE FOUNDATION FOR STUDY

In the United Presbyterian Church, for example, it is difficult to answer the question of doctrinal authority, C.T.'s question, authoritatively. The church does have a statement of belief. Yet, at many points in its history in the United States, the church has resisted movements that would make everyone conform to a set of doctrinal standards. Members of the church, except those who are ordained (ministers and officers), are not required to subscribe to any creed or statement of belief. Those who become communicant members are examined as to their beliefs. At their public reception they need only acknowledge verbally the Lordship of Jesus Christ.

But the communicant member makes a promise of action that takes the place of creedal conformity and gives an entirely different direction to what it means to be a member of the church. He promises to make "diligent use" of the Scriptures. The believer is thus made dependent on the word of God and not on his own or any other human statement of the truth. His confession of faith on becoming a communicant is not the end of learning, nor is it a sign that he has accumulated a faith that he can apply to life from then on. The church assumes that no one stops learning at that point in his church experience. It is therefore a teaching church, required to make the hearing of God's word possible. Its members are required to be perpetual students.

The broad framework within which the teaching church places itself is that of Reformed theology. Within that framework the believer, whether teacher or pupil, is free to make use of any theology or interpretation that makes a hearing of the word of God possible. The same is true of other fields of knowledge, such as linguistics or archaeology, that bear on interpretation of the Bible. The believer is free to use any and all of them to help his understanding.

Surely, in such an open-ended approach, there is one final truth at which all Christians must arrive, however much freedom they are allowed along the way. That truth is Jesus Christ. In other types of learning, "the truth" would be an abstraction or a concept, or a set of concepts, that is, a dogma or theology. To many in the church, "the truth" is one system of beliefs or statement of fundamentals. Here is yet another, and the central, difference between learning in the Christian faith and all other kinds of learning. In faith, the truth is a person, Jesus Christ, the incarnate meeting of God and man. There is no way to define and defend a truth that is confrontation and not a statement. The best that anyone can do is to let no "truths" stand in the way of the word of God and of that meeting which is faith.

The conscientious teacher ought to take up theology. He ought to expose himself to interpretations that challenge his own ideas. If he comes across a theology especially congenial to him or to his church, he can adopt it and make his teaching conform to it. But he thereby gives up being one who studies.

The teacher who is going to persevere in study holds his theology lightly, temporarily, to be challenged, corrected, reshaped by his study. The larger framework for which he is responsible should be an aid to his study and a corrective to his ideas, not the goal of understanding toward which he presses nor yet the system of thought he must enforce on the pupils. Creeds and theologies in the history of the church have been drawn up as guideposts and as correctives against extreme points of view. They point to the truth, using the disciplines of traditional insights and of new thought. However, they have often been taken as and taught as "the truth."

To put the matter another way, the teacher needs a canny knowledge of sin, beginning with his own. He recognizes that everyone resists God by putting up barriers against the hearing of God's word. He is constantly searching for such barriers in himself. Over against his understandings, which include some cherished traditional beliefs, he puts the indefinable, unprincipled truth, Jesus Christ. The teacher, because he too is one who studies, has finally no "line." He has only a method, that of his continual involvement with the Scriptures.

Give considerable time to thought or discussion about the ideas in this section. If necessary, review sections of other chapters that discuss faith. See "An Answer" in Chapter 2 and "A Parallel" in Chapter 3.

Is it true that "there is no way to define and defend a truth that is confrontation"? Jesus Christ can be defined in many ways. What are some of them? The text itself offers a definition. What is the difference between it and other definitions of Jesus Christ?

Some people, considering the responsibility of the individual Christian for study, will want to say, "Let George do it." Is being a perpetual student too much to ask of the average member of the church? Should study be, rather, the responsibility of ministers and scholars who will pass on the results of their work to members of the church? Consider this alternative in some detail. Where does it lead? If you know some church history, you should be able to recall examples of where it leads. If you are an acute observer, you should be able to cite examples of where it has led in your own church.

Theology offers a means of understanding the Bible. Theology stands under the judgment of the word of God, to be corrected by it. Both of these are guiding principles for the teacher's study. How can both of them be true?

Can the perpetual student get to the place where he has rooted out of himself all barriers to the hearing of God's word? Can he, in other words, reach sinlessness? If not, trying to locate the barriers would seem a fruitless process. Why should the teacher be concerned with them?

How do you feel about the somewhat negative way of "letting no 'truths' stand in the way of the word of God"? Should there be some more positive way to set forth the truth?

THE WAY AHEAD

The next section of this chapter is an exercise in letting no "truths" stand in the way of the word of God. Some of the common theological interpretations that teachers hold will be examined. As these ideas are brought to mind and critically examined, they will be contrasted with a suggested, temporarily adopted framework of understanding. Beyond this, what can be put over against these ideas as something positive? Nothing except the method of study itself, the continual involvement with Scripture that makes possible some hearing of the word of God.

The general framework of discussion centers in the expression *God - man,* previously used to describe faith. The words have a certain strangeness; at the same time, they seem familiar. These two words used together describe Jesus Christ. "Perfect man" and "perfect God," a less well known creed puts it.

The framework of understanding for the story of faith centers in the meeting between God and man, in Jesus Christ. The framework has two other dimensions, extending both ways in history from the central event, the coming of Christ among men. One of these dimensions is the story of the people of God before the coming of Christ. The other is the story of the people of God since the time

*of Jesus Christ, or of the church. These three dimensions
intertwine and are held together in Christ.*

THE CENTER OF THE STORY: THREE WAYS OUT

Jim Jones, Elaine Finch, and Jerry Adams are going to
be counselors at the junior high camp at Peaceful Valley.
At the planning meeting they receive the materials for
study in the camp program. Each notes with relief that
the suggestions for study are about Jesus Christ.

"Familiar ground, at last," sighs Jim, who teaches a
church school class also. He has wearied of the complexi-
ties and contradictions of the Old Testament and the
meaninglessness, to him, of church history.

"I'm so glad it's about something I know," thinks Elaine,
who has never before worked with junior highs.

"This should be simple," thinks Jerry, "something the
young people can get easily."

Are these adult workers entitled to their relief? On what
grounds have they secured it?

Jim Jones is happy because he believes that the Gospels
are the source of universal principles that can be applied
to life. Jesus Christ is the great teacher of these principles.
His life, his sayings, his parables—all teach eternal truths
that are the very basis of life.

Jim may not have given much thought to how he got
his belief; perhaps he just accepted it from his teachers or
his minister or something he read. It seemed good to him,
good enough to be his determining point of view. Back
of it lies thinking like this: We have behind us several
hundred years of Christianity, centuries of Christian civili-
zation and culture of which we Americans are the inher-
itors and, currently, the prime examples. Let us, therefore,
decide what is the essence of Christianity. We can then
draw from the New Testament the heart of Jesus Christ's
message or the ethics that have informed the Western
world. Surely this *is* the heritage that we should pass on
to our children.

A curious extension of this point of view ends in considering the New Testament as "better" or "higher" than the rest of the Bible. Indeed, Jim, along with many other Christians, thinks that the church should teach only the New Testament, meaning the Gospels. The thinking behind such an idea goes: History *ought* to have been better as a result of Christ's coming, therefore it *has been* better. We moderns can be patronizing toward Old Testament times. For example, we know that there shouldn't have been so much war. It was wrong, but people then didn't know better, because Jesus Christ hadn't come (or because they were not so civilized as we are). Using a variation of the idea, some young people explain that people in Jesus' time did not recognize him as the Son of God because they were not Christians.

The essence-of-Christianity approach offers a certain security, the security of believing that everyone today and the world in general is Christian. Christianity, not Christ, is the center of the story of faith, according to such a view. The Christianity that is meant equals the (Western) culture of today or, at least, its ideals. Many Christians hold such a view. It is also characteristic of people outside the church who are searching for common denominators between faith and other experiences of men.

There is another, more subtle security offered in reducing the New Testament to ethical principles. The possibility that moderns can be patronizing toward Old Testament times offers a hint of where the teaching of ideals usually ends. In the example given, there is a curious but typical leap of thought in the "therefore" between what ought to be and what has been. The more you teach people what they ought to do, the more they think that is what they do, regardless of what they actually do. This is known as hypocrisy. The attitude was characteristic of the Pharisees in New Testament times who were very ethical and highly tradition-centered. According to the Gospel accounts, it was one of the chief barriers to their recognizing Jesus Christ.

Using methods you have used before, try to analyze this theological view according to: the idea of faith underlying it, how it views the Bible, what it assumes about people.

Turn back to the general framework of understanding. Analyze the essence-of-Christianity approach in terms of the following questions: Where does the story of faith center? How is Jesus Christ defined? Is there a story of faith (i.e., a history involving time and place) according to the view? What place does it give to the story of the people of God before Jesus Christ? How would it view the story of the people of God since Jesus Christ? (In this work, you are seeing how a temporarily adopted larger point of view may challenge long-standing ideas.)

Consider the two examples given of the idea that the New Testament is better than the Old. Have you ever heard similar views expressed?

The text suggests one way in which a better acquaintance with the New Testament might call into question basic tenets of this approach. Those who know some church history may recognize that the view of the Old Testament as inferior to the New resembles an ancient heresy. How might a knowledge of the history of the church (the story of God's people since Jesus Christ) call into question this theological approach? (In this work, you are seeing examples of how further study may challenge long-standing ideas.)

Another kind of correction of the essence-of-Christianity view has arisen in an unexpected quarter during the past few years. When Western Christians have become acquainted with churches in other cultures (as equals now, and no longer as givers-receivers), they have been forced to see that there are other Christian traditions besides that of the West. Entirely different kinds of moral questions have to be faced in other cultures. The answers that Western Christians might quickly and automatically give, simply do not fit. The experience suggests that Western ways may not be so eternal and universal after all.

If you find that your thinking or discussion becomes very muddled, drop it and go on to the next example. You should not be concerned with whether or not you come to some one point of view. You are learning a method of work. If you can't apply it on your first try, try again.

Mrs. Finch is happy that the junior highs will be learning about Jesus Christ because she believes that the Gospels are full of spiritual lessons and will show the young people how to live spiritual lives. If anyone were to question Elaine about the meaning of spiritual lessons or spiritual values or the spiritual life, she would not be able to say very clearly what she has in mind. But she would be clear about one thing, namely, that the spiritual is very much needed in the world today.

The origins of Elaine's view are not so vague as her ideas. They lie in the beginnings of church history and lead to what was once held to be a heresy. According to an ancient and non-Biblical view, the worldly and the spiritual were two separate and opposed things. Sometimes the opposites were described as the bodily and the spiritual. Everything worldly was bad; the spiritual was the only good. Many Christians today hold essentially the same view. In later times a psychological refinement was added, positing in human beings a spiritual part to which God, being spirit, could speak. Probably many who hold the spiritual view today have some such idea in mind. They continue to think that anything other than the spiritual is bad, so bad that God can have nothing to do with it.

The spiritual view isolates faith from the world and from the reality of bodily existence. On such grounds it is difficult to see what it could be concerned with, other than prayer and meditation. In times past it has, and in some faiths today is, concerned mostly with the life to come. Spiritualism then becomes a kind of perfectionism that can reach expression only beyond this world. Spiritual teaching, in actual practice, comes down about where the essence-of-Christianity approach comes down—in ethical principles.

There is some security in believing in a spiritual realm or a spiritual compartment in the psyche. It is a convenient filing place for things that might disturb life in other compartments. For example, a businessman need never bother himself with the morality of his methods if all such questions belong to the spiritual and have nothing to do with the real world of business. Similarly, a church devoted to the spiritual may never need to concern itself with the pleas of a minority group for simple justice in its community. Such matters lie entirely outside its view.

Test the vagueness of the spiritual approach by asking several people what they mean by spiritual experiences, values, teachings. What is usually meant by the spiritual life?

Many people have difficulty with the picture of Jesus spitting on the ground, and mixing spit and clay to put on a blind man's eyes (Mark 8:23; John 9:6). "That's not the Jesus I know!" they say. What Jesus do they know? Why is it difficult to imagine that Jesus could and did spit?

The interpretation of the word "spirit" as used in the Bible offers an example of how further study on a scholarly level can challenge long-held views. In recent years theologians and Bible scholars have given a great deal of attention to the Hebrew language (the language of the Old Testament) and to the ways it influenced the use of Greek in the writing of the New Testament. For many centuries, the meaning of spirit was interpreted in the context of the Greek idea of world versus spirit, from which was derived the theory of a separate compartment or faculty in man. However, studies in Biblical language suggest that "spirit" in its original meaning cannot be separated from the body and cannot be thought of as the good opposed to the evil. Look up the word in several Bible dictionaries old and new.

Analyze the spiritual view according to its idea of faith, its view of the Bible, its assumptions about persons.

Look up the heresy in early church times related to the spiritual view. How does knowing about this development in church history help you assess the spiritual approach?

Consider this view in the light of the general framework suggested in "The Way Ahead." What is at the center of the story of faith? How would Jesus Christ be defined? Is there a story of faith? How would the story of the people of God before Christ be considered? What view would be held of the story of the church?

Can you think of other examples of how the spiritual view isolates faith from the world?

Jerry Adams is happy to study the story of Jesus Christ because he believes it offers practical lessons that each junior high can apply to his life right now. Jesus himself is the example for their lives. The one thing Jerry wants to do is to end each session with something simple that will show the young people how to live. He wants the Bible to apply to their lives. (A good question is, How did the Bible and life come to be so far apart that one has to be applied to the other?)

The something simple is always a matter of individual morality. It is likely to be what the young person should do in school on Monday, or with his friends on Tuesday, or at the game on Wednesday. Any larger questions, such as the value placed on education in our society or the carefully class-segregated (if not color-segregated) nature of the school, Jerry and other teachers consider to be inappropriate for the consideration of young believers. When it is suggested that young people concern themselves with the possibility of total annihilation, teachers raise strong objections. They would prefer that each session end with a practical lesson, such as not cheating, honoring mothers, or the nonpaying nature of crime.

The emphasis is on the individual conscience and its perfecting. The view combines elements of the essence of Christianity and the spiritual approaches, and comes out at about the same place, except that it is more interested in specific actions than in principles. What matters is that the Christian should be right in himself. So long as he is, history, commerce, and the world can go on their way. It is somehow dirty and degrading to faith to be concerned with such things. What is disregarded is the fact that many who believe this way are very much—up to sixteen hours a day—concerned with commerce, for example.

In a theoretical way the individual Christian, properly built up by his moral calisthenics, is supposed to influence the world in which he lives. He usually thinks he does so by being a good example. Turning the idea about, Jesus is made to be the great example. Anyone who studies the Gospels with a mind free from an idealized portrait of Jesus Christ may well wonder whether it is a good thing to want young people to be like him. Therefore, many idealized portraits have been devised. Jesus Christ is the original businessman, the ideal American, the Great Scout, the most popular man of all time.

Like the essence-of-Christianity view, the individual-morality approach centers in and teaches a particular pattern of living. It cuts itself off from any source of judgment on that pattern. It too leads to a subtle kind of hypocrisy that can be observed in many a junior high class. The teacher who presses for an application to life reaches the point of highest satisfaction when he can do so. That moment is frequently the point of greatest boredom for junior highs. They will be polite enough to accept advice and even to proffer examples of what they should do, but they are usually saying what the teacher wants them to say. The lessons are too simple for them to concern themselves very much. Meantime they are being shown a time-honored way of evading the word of God by retreating into individual righteousness. Both the prophets of Old Testament times and Jesus accused the people of God of being great on self-righteousness (and its attendant piety), but weak on such matters as justice and mercy.

The most common plea that teachers make is for something which the junior highs can "apply to life." What is meant by this plea?

Consider the idea of Jesus as an example for young people. Would you honestly want them to be like him, remembering that he had no home, never married or fathered children, was rude to the best people of his time, was executed as a common criminal? Discussion of such questions will reveal what idealized portraits of Jesus you hold.

A member of an adult class studying the Gospel of Luke says, "Oh, I just think if we could have been there then, seen how attractive and popular Jesus was, been drawn to him along with the crowds—why, it would be easy to believe in him!" What's wrong with this idea in terms of the Gospel accounts of Jesus' ministry?

Analyze the individual-morality approach in the way you analyzed the others.

Why are the "lessons too simple" for junior highs to concern themselves with? Why do you think such lessons are satisfying to the teacher?

THE CENTER OF THE STORY: A CORRECTIVE

If Jim and Elaine and Jerry are very sure of themselves, they will probably look at the study materials once or twice before camp begins, enough to get in mind the Bible passages to be taken up. Then they will develop the material each in his own predecided way. Suppose, instead, they look more closely at their study materials. They may find other interpretations than their own. Somewhere the interpretations may openly identify and call into question the very ideas they hold. They may or may not recognize the challenge to their beliefs. If they do, they are going to feel uncomfortable. The discomfort will lead them either to become more entrenched in their own ideas or to think more deeply.

In a time that values faith as peace of mind, is it fair to disturb teachers in such a way? Why is it done? Is it merely a matter of someone else's opinions' being put against those of the teacher? And, finally, isn't everyone free to work out his own beliefs?

The answer is that responsible teaching materials will always challenge the teacher's beliefs. They will present a larger framework of understanding that, many times, will sound new and different to the teacher. If responsible people produce the materials, it will not be a matter of opinions alone. And the responsible teacher will challenge his own ideas and push himself to think, just as he challenges young adolescents to think. Yes, everyone is free to work out his own beliefs, but no Christian is free to do so without involvement with the Scriptures.

The three camp counselors could all claim that they put Jesus Christ at the center of faith. They are likely to feel that, as long as you teach Jesus Christ, the Old Testament is unnecessary or is an extra, and the history of the church is irrelevant. The Christ they teach tends to become timeless and universal or the representative of current values and cultures, because all three teachers interpret Jesus Christ outside the story of faith. How will more involvement with the story of faith (a larger framework of understanding) tend to challenge or correct the views of these adults?

The story of faith begins with one man called by God, moves on to tell about a family, then a rescued group of tribes that becomes a nation, and finally a broken, conquered people. Throughout their story these people were called to make God known in the world; they had a mission different from that of any other people or nation. Then the story of faith tells about One who took the place of the people who failed in their mission. Through him there came into being a new people of God, no longer a family by blood relationship or a nation, but a people of all nationalities, existing within the world as a family in Jesus Christ.

Jesus Christ has to be interpreted in terms that come out of the history of the people whose place he took. In one way, the fact is obvious. A glance at the Gospels shows many references to Moses, David, Elijah, and others, and quotations from writings now included in the Old Testament. The teacher needs some knowledge of the history of God's people even to study New Testament passages with understanding.

Beyond references and quotations there is the matter of patterns of meaning. Part of the problem here is the, by now, familiar one of the differences in language—that is, ways of thinking—between ancient times and modern times. The people of Old Testament times did not think in terms of principles applied to life. They did not recognize the existence of conscience. Spirit, to them, was not separate from body. Earthly, material things were not considered evil. Individuality was not highly regarded. The people of God were to be his servants, not the other way around. Principles, conscience, spirit, the importance of the individual, and God as the agent of successful man are patterns in the language of modern life. Such ways of thinking come into conflict with those of the Bible. The responsible teacher has to engage himself in that conflict.

A question can be raised as to whether it is necessary to recapture the language and thought patterns of Old Testament times. Are they not, after all, too primitive to have any relevance today? Has not mankind progressed immeasurably since then? Different answers could be made to such questions. But there is something more beyond the language of the Bible; it is the matter of how God works.

For example, few things in the story of faith are more disturbing to modern ways of thinking than the fact that God chose one people through whom to make himself known. Why didn't he make himself known to everyone? Modern explanations of the chosen people are numerous. The most popular is that the ancient Hebrews were endowed with a genius for religion. Another is that the Hebrews suffered from an illusion, whereas God himself was more democratic.

Here is an example of conflict between interpretations, one from the story of faith, the other from modern ideas. The Biblical witness is that God worked through one people within historical situations and within time to make himself known in the world. According to modern thinking, such a thing is unthinkable. God works in more general and timeless ways. He makes himself known to anyone who searches for him, and he certainly would not play favorites like that. The Biblical witness would answer that favoritism was no part of the matter; being a chosen people meant, finally, bearing a cross. Well, then, modern ideas counter, there is a psychological explanation: they had a gift for religion or they had delusions of grandeur, perhaps a persecution complex. At any rate, it is ridiculous to think that the almighty and eternal God was so concerned with the history of one obscure, unsuccessful people several thousand years ago.

Anyone who lives in the modern era thinks and breathes psychology, democracy, success, God as the Father of all, and the value of religion. It is not a question of whether these are good or bad, adequate or inadequate, patterns of thought. The question is, What happens when they are the only viewpoints used in interpreting the Bible? The person who uses them exclusively finds a way around the uncomfortable aspects of the story of faith. When he takes such a way, he makes the Bible less offensive. He also attempts to lessen the difference between God and man, and to put God at a safe distance as a general, impassive sort of god. An adequate barrier has been put up; he will never be surprised by insights from the story of faith.

But the Christian who is responsible for involvement with the Scripture has to let it speak to him. When Biblical patterns of thought conflict with accepted ways of thinking, he cannot take easy ways out. He must pause, think, consider, weigh. In short, he must be one who studies. And, if he is a responsible teacher, he is also one who handles Scripture rightly, that is, with some faithfulness to its own nature.

Recall how each of the "three ways out" would describe Jesus Christ. How much are the descriptions based on modern patterns of thought? How much are they influenced by Biblical ways of thought? Consider how such views might be questioned from an understanding of Jesus Christ in the context of the story of faith. For example, what is the difference between "Jesus the original businessman," and Jesus, God's suffering servant?

The bulletin board outside a church carried this statement: "'God so loved the world.' Do you?" Most Christians would immediately react by thinking, "But I'm not *supposed* to love the world!" What traditional view lies behind such a feeling? How does it differ from the Biblical view?

In understanding the controversy between Jesus and the Pharisees over the law (and its continuation in Paul's writings), what differences would there be between: interpreting "law" according to its modern definition, and interpreting "law" according to its meaning in the Old Testament?

What are some other points at which the Biblical view of things is offensive to modern ideas? Recall insights from the story of Joseph taken up in Chapter 4, as one example.

The argument of God's way of working can be used to support many things. Sometimes it can be called on to validate a meaningless miracle that is clearly a piece of legendizing in Bible material. (The "corrective" here lies in the meaning of signs and wonders and the question of whether God ever used mighty works merely to show men what he could do or to demand blind belief,) Or "We can't explain it—that's just God's way of working," can be used to support the idea that the people God chose are superior to others. (What corrective does the story of God's people offer to this idea?)

Can what is said here about the conflict between Biblical ways of thought and modern ideas be used to support the view that Christians must believe the world is flat, as the ancients did? Why or why not?

THE PEOPLE OF GOD VS. THE INDIVIDUALIST

Of the three camp counselors, the one who will cling most persistently to his point of view is Jerry, who holds to the individual-morality approach. A number of factors contribute to his persistence. One is the fact that teachers tend to teach as they were taught. Chances are, Jerry was taught that point of view by his teachers, and Jerry's teachers were so taught, and the teachers of Jerry's teachers were so taught, and so on back about one hundred and fifty years.

The chances of this being true are good, because, almost from its beginnings, the Sunday school had a semiofficial theology directed toward individual morality. It was a widely held view of faith and not the exclusive possession of the Sunday school, but Sunday schools specialized in it. Most teachers would have denied that they held any theology at all. They rather prided themselves on being practical (more practical than the church, which was something else again), and, therefore, on coming up with unmistakable and applicable lessons. The Bible, they believed, was being taught without interpretation.

Furthermore, Jerry's point of view nowadays is backed up by some approaches that have discarded the nineteenth-century morality that nineteenth-century teachers inevitably taught. What is essentially the same approach is now directed toward character training, successful living, and peace of mind. Beyond the church the idea that the purpose of faith is to make people good is widely accepted and so loudly acclaimed that most churches are forced to conform to it.

There is also common sense. Is it not true in the final analysis that there is no faith except as an individual person has faith and that nothing is changed unless an individual person is changed? And Jerry can find some comfort in the description of faith as the hidden existence of the individual person under God. Finally, what can possibly be wrong or questionable about wanting people to be good?

The question is, Good for what? For the self-satisfaction of having a good conscience? For the continued guilt of a too-demanding conscience? For the hope that God helps those, and only those, who help themselves be good? For the hypocrisy of the Pharisees? For the exalted position of being an example? Are any of these what faith is all about?

In the story of faith the people of God were called to be good for the world. They certainly were required to be righteous, which may be something different from being good. The reason for their righteousness was their mission to the world; they were to be "that different people" who could make God known. But righteousness easily turns into being good, and the people of God subverted it. Being good became keeping the rules and ignoring the law, or word, of God. The satisfied conscience, the hope of special status with God, the exaltation of being an example —the good, religious people of Jesus' time had them all. What they had lost sight of was not being good, but the righteousness of God and the world they were called to serve.

However much faith is the hidden existence of the individual person with God, the subject matter of the story of faith is not the individual believer and his conscience. It is the story of God's people and the world. The three dimensions of the story of faith—the time before Christ, the coming of Christ, and the history of the church—focus on the people of God and the world for which they are to be good. The people of God today are also called to be in the world as those who make God known. The pursuit of being good is not the way to the world, but one way out of it.

Here is yet another reason why study proposes to let go the inner life of the person under God. The spiritual development or pious exercises or conscience-flexing athletics of the individual are improper concerns for study. So are the community life of the church and all introspection or dynamic experiments about the church's groupness and interrelationships among its members. The focus of study is objective (as is also its reason for being undertaken): it is the relationship of the people of God to the world.

For one thing, this means that the teacher should arm himself with some awareness of the distinctions between the people of God and the world in which they live. His resources, again, are the Biblical ways of looking at such things as the call of God to a people, the intrusive and unexpected nature of God's revelation of himself, and a sense of the prophetic, that is, self-critical nature of the people of God. With some such insights, the teacher can approach with suspicion any views that seem to make the church or faith look the same as everything or anything else in the world. Such views are numerous. One is the idea that everyone worships the same god, the god of his choice, under different names. Another is the belief that every man searches for God. Still another is that religion is good and the Christian faith is a religion. Then there is the view of God as the summation and deification of all that is good in human experience. And there are pressures on the church to add motivation to such things as the schools' character-training program and community and national goals.

But while the teacher is drawing the line in this way, he also needs to resist the temptation to withdraw young people from the world as those who must keep themselves clean from it. Most church schools teach as though the pupils would be enclosed in the world of the church all their lives. Thus attendance at church is considered a proper outcome of faith, Laymen's (or Youth) Sunday is a demonstration of how much laymen can act like ministers, and commitment to a church vocation is the highest possible outcome of teaching.

What is needed, rather, is more concern with the world, from a certain point of view, more worldliness.

Chances are that you, like Jerry, were taught from the individual-morality point of view. You will, therefore, have difficulty in isolating it and looking at it.

How common is the idea that the purpose of faith is to make people good and that the Bible is about being good? Suppose you asked members of a typical Sunday morning congregation whether or not they agreed with the idea. What percentage of them would raise their hands to signify "yes"? What different variations of the idea have you heard or read recently?

Recall some of the persons of Old Testament times through whom God worked: Abraham, Moses, David, the prophets. Were they "good" people?

What is the difference between righteousness and being good? Must the effort to be good always end in hypocrisy?

"Spirit" is a good word to study closely as a clue to the difference between Biblical views and common views. The Holy Spirit today is widely held to be God speaking to the individual. He is associated with prayer, meditation, worship, inspiration, and certain vague feelings. Using a concordance, study a sampling of the acts of the Holy Spirit in the book of The Acts and in some of the letters. Is the focus of the Spirit toward the individual's pious development?

Emphasis on the mission of the people of God can change the reading of the story of faith. It might also change church teaching, which today is directed, for the most part, toward the good individual. In what ways? "Mission" here means something different from its common definition as a part of the church's responsibility delegated to missionaries and missionary societies and a section of the church budget.

What dangers are there in viewing the church as different from the world to which it is called? What are some other interpretations, made by the church and by the world around it, that make it seem the same as everything and anything else?

"More concern with the world" means many things to many people. If you are working with a group of teachers, find out what it means to each of them. Keep these views in mind as you study the next section, which is about the third dimension of the story of faith, the history of the church.

THE PEOPLE OF GOD AND THE WORLD

"I don't know enough!" is the cry of many a teacher when it is suggested that study of the history of the church is essential in teaching faith. He is probably right, but he is also saying some other things. The teacher who agrees with the three camp counselors might also mean that the church, while maybe a necessary thing, detracts from the spiritual purity of Jesus' message. He likes to teach from the Gospels, not only because they are familiar ground, but because they can be made to support the leap from Jesus to universal ethics. The book of The Acts and the letters do not lend themselves to such a leap of understanding, so he ignores them. Most teachers take a detour around the entire course of church history because they suppose that God works in the world through the individual conscience and not through the new people of God. Finally, they would and do say, it is difficult to draw from church history any lessons for the individual pupil to take to heart.

The history of the church is the history of God at work in the world through the body of Christ, the new people called to serve him. It differs from the story of faith in Scriptures, because it looks back to the Bible. In a certain sense, as the new people of God, the church continues the story. But early in its life, the church closed the Scriptures, thereby declaring its dependence on events of the past as determinative and the record of them as the means of God's speaking to his people.

Church history is the account of how the new people of God have turned back to the story of faith and what they have made of the word of God in their times. It is a history of Biblical interpretation. Such a statement can suggest the dullest kind of study, tracking down the successive scholars of the church and their theological controversies. What is meant, however, is the Biblical interpretation made in the lives of lay people.

For certain specialists in the church a study of Thomas Aquinas' logic, for example, may be appropriate. That was one type of Biblical interpretation made in the past. For the people of God, who are by and large not scholars or specialists, what would be important about Thomas Aquinas' time would appear in answer to such questions as: How did lay people believe and act then? How was the word of God received? What view of faith did they have according to what we can perceive in their ways of practicing it? What barriers did they put between themselves and the word? Or, in some cases, what barriers did others put up?

In the answers to such questions, Christians of the present can identify their own interpretations of the word of God also, provided they give up any idea of progress or perfection. If they see the church as a growing institution more perfect or somewhat better today than it was, they merely use their own interpretations of the word as a vantage point from which to judge the past. They may easily see that every representation and interpretation of the word of God made in the past was, in a sense, "imperfect" when measured by the word itself. They will also see that the same is true of any interpretations made in the present, representations they themselves are making as the people of God. Thus Christians today put themselves alongside lay people of other times in an effort to correct themselves by a fresh hearing of the word of God. And the "lesson" of church history is solely turning again to the word to hear and to venture forth in faith into the world.

As with either Jesus Christ or the story of God's people before him, it is possible to take the history of the church out of the context of the story of faith. One teacher will take a cultural approach to church history, for example, making it merely additional information to the general history of the West. Another will see the church as a human institution with a history similar to that of other groupings in society, a history of dates, events, persons, heroes, and leaders. Sometimes the church's own tradition of worship, art, and the like is considered a heritage to be passed on. All these views take church history out of the context of God at work among men whom he has called to make himself known in the world, men interpreting and representing the word of God in their own times.

The general methods of study, discussed in Chapter 4 in relation to the story of faith in the Bible, remain the same. Identification, now with the lay people of the church, is still the basic method. There is also need for development of the historical situation not in the broad terms of historical movements, but in terms of the lives of people of other times. Bible material is used as the touchstone of comparison and correction, instead of being the central story to be taken up. For that reason the interpretive documents of the early church, the New Testament letters, are most often used. But the direction of study is still toward the story of faith in the Scriptures and toward the Christian's dependence on it as God's way of speaking to him.

Such an approach offers clues to what is meant by the focus on the people of God and their relationship to the world. For one thing, it means that all study with young adolescents must be within the dual context of the church and the world. However much it may be right to shelter little children within the church, these same children cannot be sheltered in it always. At some point they must be the people of God called to his work in the dangers, potentialities, falsenesses, philosophies, hopelessnesses, hopes, and fears of the present time.

This does not mean a simple process of bringing the world's problems to the Scriptures for answers, any more than study means bringing the young person's problems to the Bible. Neither does it mean offering to young people the hope of making the world over. In Biblical terms, it means "the equipment of the saints for the work of ministry."

At the very least, it will require locating young people as members of that community called out of the world and put back in it as those who have heard God speak. It means involvement with the Scripture and involvement with the world as that which God loves. Such a view of the church, as the self-offering ministry of lay people to the world, is so different from common views that no one can now say all it will mean for the church's work of study. It leaves many unanswered questions that ought to be explored constantly by every group of adults working with young adolescents.

Common views of "more concern with the world" are: Christians are to make it over into the Kingdom of God; the Bible gives answers to the world's problems; every session must show how faith relates to the world today; each Christian must be equipped to buttonhole his neighbors and fellow workers and talk to them like an evangelist; Christians must learn how to get more people into the church; there are certain Christian attitudes toward social problems that must be learned. Consider each of these in the light of clues suggested here about the people of God in relationship to the world.

Can Christians of today hope to profit from the mistakes of the past and make a perfect interpretation of God's word to the world? Why or why not?

Why shouldn't the church teach about its history simply so that Christians will know something about church history?

In addition to being in touch with the Biblical world, the teacher of young adolescents needs to be in touch with the world today. Which world—the nineteenth-century world that the Sunday school tradition tries to keep him in touch with, the world as he knows it, the world into which young adolescents are growing up? What differences are there between these last two?

What are some of the unanswered questions brought up by the different view of the church as a self-offering ministry of lay people to the world? List some and put them on an agenda for discussion by teachers of young adolescents. For some further implications, see *The Young Adolescent in the Church.*

You may want to reread this chapter and reconsider some of the challenges it puts to your own views. If you are studying with other teachers, discussion of this chapter may take several meetings and may seem more muddling than enlightening (which is how it should be).

6. Homework—the Teacher's

*How can the adult prepare for
work with young adolescents?*

AROUND AND ABOUT

The boys are off to school. Don has gone to the office. The baby is asleep. Adelaide is washing breakfast dishes. "It *is* funny," she thinks, meaning an idea she read in a book about the church. The writer had suggested that the church was really, or might better be, an underground organization with, so far as the world was concerned, subversive aims. Adelaide is thinking how Elder Bacon in her church would react to the idea, because he is always finding subversives everywhere. But for herself, Adelaide finds the idea thought-provoking. How would it be, she muses, off on a tangent again, if she enrolled all the junior highs in her class in a secret society? They'd love it! But seriously, what was the writer trying to say? How could he suggest that the church be an underground movement when its most striking symbol was the spire in the middle of town?

Tonight Irv's desk is covered with books, magazines, a notebook, and a Bible, as well as the usual report sheets and lunch pail. He is reading about the prophet Elijah hiding away from Jezebel and from a threat to his life. Irv looks up and scans the darkened reaches of the steel mill where he works as night watchman. Dim lights shine here and there. His office is an island of light in the shadows, his refuge. He thinks how it would be to hear a voice calling him out. He turns back to read how God called the prophet out of his hiding place to put before him the powerful forces of nature and, finally, to speak to him in the still small voice.

"It's Dot," comes a voice over the phone, so Mary sits down. This will be a long conversation. Dot is in charge of the new junior high program, a combination of what used to be church school and a fairly defunct fellowship. They meet on Wednesdays after school. With a new kind of schedule the six adult leaders are more or less playing it by ear. It is a joke among them that every time they begin to know what they are doing Dot comes along with a new idea. "I've been reading the next unit," says Dot. Mary makes an indefinite noise such as might be taken to mean that she has too. Inwardly she resolves that she will read the unit right away. "Well, I was wondering," Dot continues . . .

"Coffee, sir?" asks the stewardess. Al looks up from several centuries back. Gradually the interior of the plane replaces a sixteenth-century English cottage, and Al becomes again a Super Company representative on Flight 608. "Oh, yes, thank you," he says. He has been trying to imagine how eighth-graders in his church school class will react to putting themselves in the place of people hearing the Bible for the first time. They were people who had learned their faith from tradition and by having it passed on from others. Now they were going back to the source for the first time. An interesting possibility, thinks Al, because most of the young people he knows are in the same position. Everything they know about faith amounts to what someone has told them or what everyone else believes. Sometimes they are positively jolted when they go back to the source. Yes, well, so is Al himself at times.

"If nobody minds," says Thelma, "I'd like to work with the group preparing the interview of Abraham. I had some ideas while I was going over that." The other teachers in the junior high department agree. Other work groups are planned and teachers assigned to them. They plan a tentative time when all the junior highs will watch the interview prepared by Thelma's group. After that, some of the teachers are to take small groups of junior highs to talk over the interview and to do some reading in the Bible. With the schedule for Sunday morning more or less planned, the teachers look up the Bible references they will be using. They talk over what they read, bringing in ideas from the background material each has studied before the meeting. Together they work out some possible questions to develop as they imagine the junior highs discussing the same material. When the meeting breaks up rather late, Thelma goes home with two things yet to prepare for the session. One is the guidance of the interview work group. The other consists of the specific questions she will use in the reading-discussion group.

They are all sitting on the ground and it is a warm early summer day. That is why Lucille squirms. Better get used to it, she thinks. She tries to concentrate on the camp manual and the suggestions for discussion in a small group of junior highs. She and all the other leaders are reading it over and will discuss the different ideas to see how they could carry them out in camp two weeks from now. They are spending the day at the campsite. "Now, let me see," Lucille thinks, as a breeze ruffles the pages of her Bible, "that was chapter 4 in Mark."

Irene stops in at the church while she is downtown. In the audio-visual room she threads a filmstrip into a projector and quickly looks at eight frames about the prophet Isaiah that she plans to use in the junior high class. She goes over the script that she will read with the frames. On the back of her shopping list she makes notes of some questions to ask before and after the frames are shown and hopes she will not lose the slip of paper. She leaves

word for the audio-visual director to place the projector
and a tabletop screen in her classroom. I'd better get here
extra early, thinks Irene as she leaves the church.

The pop bottles are certainly getting in the way. Any
minute, thinks Sandra, one is going to go over right on my
living room rug. It seems most likely when Ted gives a
sudden jump backward. He is trying to act his surprise
on hearing a fellow disciple report that they have seen and
talked to Jesus after his death. Four of the junior highs
are preparing the dramatized scene for the class. Sandra
suggests that all the actors sit down and look at the Bible
passages again, trying to imagine how they would feel
if they were actually the persons involved.

"Honey, do we have any shelf paper?" Lyall comes into
the kitchen armed with a black crayon snitched from little
Lyall's toy box. "I want to make a word list." "A what?"
says Honey. "Well, you know, those kids—in Sunday
school, I mean—are always getting stopped by some word
or other in the Bible. So it says here to make a list of them
and put it up so they can look at it. I thought it was a good
idea. Got any shelf paper?"

Vivian is reading an editorial about breaking the law.
Civil rights demonstrators are unlawful, the editorial
claims, and show a high disregard for laws. It is a hot
issue just now. Vivian remembers reading an article in
her denominational magazine that had raised the issue
from another point of view, that of the responsibility of
Christians to a higher law. The article had suggested that
there were times when Christians had to resist existing
laws. Vivian begins to recall bits and pieces of conversation in her ninth-grade class about Jesus and his not keeping the law and what kind of law it was and how the
Pharisees were law-abiding. "H'm-m," thinks Vivian. She
tears out the editorial and then goes to look for the other
article.

They have moved the church librarian's desk down to the first-floor hall where almost everyone passes it sometime or other. That makes it easier for Ralph, and harder. "Uh, I want," he says to the lady at the desk, "something that tells, uh, when the book of Ephesians was written, and things like that." Ralph notes that she does not think it such a stupid question. She turns to one of the bookcases and brings out a fairly large book. "I think this will have what you want," she says as she begins thumbing through pages. "Yes, here, and the next few pages." Ralph signs the book out and takes it home.

Someone snaps on the room lights as the last frame of the filmstrip and the music fade away. Dave, the superintendent of the junior high department, stands before the group of teachers. "As you know," he says, "when classes start in two weeks we will be taking up the story that the Bible tells. According to the way this filmstrip presented it, what would you say the Bible is about?" "I'm new at this," says Clarke, "so I suppose everyone else knew this, but I was interested in the way the film shows it is all one story. The most I can remember from what I was taught about the Bible is a bunch of stories and teachings." "I thought it was interesting the way they wove in information about how the Bible was written," says Estelle. "Say, Dave, the kids would like to see that, wouldn't they?" No one had yet answered Dave's question, but that was all right. They were all beginning to think about the year ahead, and that was what Dave had hoped the filmstrip would start them doing.

The children are in bed. Jane is out to a meeting. Brad pours the last cup of warmed-over supper coffee and slumps down in a corner of the sofa. He reads over some notes scribbled in the margins of the teacher's material for his junior high class. The notes are more or less verbatim records of comments made by members of the class last Sunday. They had been studying the time Jesus drove the money changers out of the Temple. Brad noted that one boy, Ed, had taken to the idea of Jesus' dramatically upsetting the established customs of his time. Ed's comments had been somewhat guarded but nevertheless showed that such a revolutionary action appealed to him. Alice and Jean had reacted strongly when the junior highs contrasted the angry Jesus revealed in the incident with the usual sweet, gentle pictures of Jesus. They were going to stick with the sweet and gentle. Tim said that he thought perhaps Jesus harmed his cause in such a violent gesture. Why was it, Tim wanted to know, that Jesus never tried in a gentle, persuasive way to win over the Pharisees? Debbie recalled the story of Nicodemus, saying that it showed he had. Then Anne rather tentatively expressed her feeling that Jesus seemed conceited. He always brought everything back to himself, she pointed out. Brad had left this an open question, knowing that it was an inescapable one in the coming sessions. But he noted that most of the junior highs agreed with Anne's judgment.

All these adults are preparing for study with young adolescents. They are preparing in general or for a specific session. Most of them are making preparations alone; some are working with other adults. In one case, the planning ahead includes junior highs at work also.

What different kinds of preparation are described in the episodes in this section? List them. Which ones are similar to what you do in preparation?

Preparation for study begins with an adult who studies, one who has undertaken for himself the obligation to study and to challenge his own ideas. This type of study is outlined in Chapter 5. The reason for the adult's study should be not merely the next session he is to guide but his own obligation to involvement with Scripture.

Keep a finger or a bookmark in the first page of this chapter. You will be referring to the episodes given there many times as you read on.

THE MATTER OF TIME

The teacher's preparation for the work of study with young adolescents takes time. "How much time?" someone is sure to ask, "For each hour of class time," the efficient one will want to know, "how much time should I spend in preparation?" Wouldn't it be fine if it were possible to work out a formula for everyone: x hours of preparation for y hours of study with pupils. Each teacher has to work out his own formula. But one thing is sure, x exceeds y by many times.

Truth to tell, there is some ambiguity about this matter of time. Those who recruit teachers for the church are often anxious to represent the work in the easiest possible terms. They may even tell the prospective teacher that he need give only an hour a week and a little extra time. Perhaps the new teacher has taught before in the not-too-distant past. He recalls that then he could get by with fifteen minutes or so on Saturday night for looking over the lesson. Even if he has never taught, he probably knows that the Saturday night glance has been the traditional way of preparing for Sunday school.

Someone should come right out and say it: those days are gone forever. (And church school recruiters should be honest and daring enough to ask more than a few minutes of new teachers.) Most denominational curricula demand more than a few minutes of preparation. They do so because they represent an approach that takes seriously the task of teaching. It is still possible to get materials of the old kind, mostly from nondenominational publishers, but users of them have to pay the price of taking their theology along with their ease of use.

Preparation does take time. If the work of study is worth undertaking at all, then there is no way around the need for time. In the following suggestions the number of hours of preparation will be at its maximum, because all the possible things a teacher might do will be presented. Probably no one teacher would do all these things. Some of them, though they seem to require more time than any teacher thinks he can give, are in reality timesaving suggestions.

How common is the Saturday-night-glance approach to preparation?

How would you fill in the formula, x hours of preparation for y hours of classwork? What do x and y equal in your case?

Planning Ahead for the Year

Dave, the superintendent of the junior high department, shows a filmstrip about the Bible to help teachers begin to think about the year ahead. These teachers use materials planned on a yearly theme. Thus they are able to do advance planning that pays off in efficiency and time-saving as the year proceeds. Probably they are meeting in late summer or early fall before the beginning of the church school teaching year, planned in most churches to coincide with the opening of the public school year. The superintendent and / or teachers might plan other kinds of meetings as preparation for the year. In addition, there are steps that each teacher can take to plan ahead.

However, there are two large "ifs" to take into account. Planning ahead is possible if the adult worker knows in advance that he is to work with young adolescents and is not asked on the twenty-seventh of September to start working the first Sunday in October. And if the materials for the fall quarter (or for the year) are available to him several weeks in advance and are not handed to him the first Sunday he reports for work. These ifs are more or less beyond the control of teachers. There is nothing teachers can do about the first one. About the second there may be something they can do. By late summer the teaching materials are probably on hand but, like everything else about the church school, they are caught in a summertime slump. Besides, most ordering secretaries or others responsible for materials have never heard of anything but the Saturday-night-glance system of preparation, so there is no hurry. The enterprising teacher might get his materials early by picking locks and breaking open packages or, perhaps, by respectfully asking for them.

Planning ahead for the year has two main aspects. One is previewing; the other is getting organized for teaching.

PREVIEWING

Alex Forman is an old hand in the junior high department, it being his third year as teacher of the eighth-grade class. The first Sunday after the Formans return from their August vacation Alex stops in the church school office to get the teaching materials he will be using when classes begin in September. "Want to get an early start," he says to the secretary of supplies.

Alex gets his early start one evening when the rest of the family are out. He digs out the new materials from the pile of magazines on the coffee table. He sits down on the sofa and casually looks through the materials. Soon he gets up and moves over to the desk to find a pencil. He begins underlining and making notes in the materials.

The curriculum Alex uses is developed with an annual theme. Therefore the fall quarter material includes introduction and interpretation of the year's theme. These are the items that Alex is looking for and marking. He may find:

—an article describing the general approach to be taken.

—descriptions of the tools that the curriculum provides for use, such as pupil's reading book, notebook, and the like.

—an outline of the year's work.

—a list of outside resources that would help him think further about the subject of study.

The outside resources might include denominationally prepared materials intended to help the teacher do some prior, broad-scale study. For example, there may be a study guide for individual reading or group study. A filmstrip (such as the one used by Dave for the teachers meeting) is an example of another curriculum-related resource. It will be listed chiefly for use in class but might also be used by a group of teachers as introduction to the year's work. In addition, there may be suggestions of other books related to the theme.

Alex may or may not have time to delve into these additional resources. But the suggestion of a study guide for group discussion sets him thinking. He makes a note to ask Dave, the superintendent, whether the junior high teachers could do something like that. He jots down the name of a book he hopes to borrow from the church library and hopes to get time to look at it in the next few weeks.

The things that Alex has been searching out are all related to the subject matter of study. Some of them suggest preparation that he can do alone and quickly, such as reading the interpretive article and going over the outline. Others might better be done with other teachers. Alex has never bothered much with teachers meetings. He found them rather dull and pointless. But maybe with a new superintendent taking over things will be different. Alex decides to call Dave and sound him out about the possibility of teachers doing some study together.

It turns out that Dave is a few jumps ahead of the teacher. He too has been thinking about the year ahead. His plan is to have a teachers meeting and show the filmstrip related to the year's theme. In that way, he figures, teachers can get a preview of the entire year as well as get acquainted with a tool they might use in classwork.

Alex and Dave are on the right track because preparation in subject terms should be the major item both for the individual teacher and for teachers meetings at the beginning of the year.

GETTING ORGANIZED

However, Alex has some organizational matters on his mind which he would like to see taken up by the junior high teachers. He has been mulling these matters over ever since he was fishing one day during vacation. For no reason that he could fathom, an old grudge suddenly rose up out of the water and the stillness. The grudge was sweet little Miss Gill who, every Sunday that he can remember has opened his classroom door and come in saying: "Good morning, Mr. Forman, boys and girls. Isn't this a lovely day? Do you have the attendance book? Have you put the cards in the right pocket? The cards for absentees go here, you know. Oh, thank you."

Alex can no longer count the times this routine has seriously upset what was going on in class. He has nothing against Miss Gill, or at least he tries not to have. She seems to him merely the symbol of a clash of purposes. He wants to teach and he wants time to teach. But the more he thinks about it, the more things he can list that make it difficult. All these things which stand in the way of teaching are precisely the items taken up at the regular teachers meetings over and over again. Maybe that is why he just doesn't care to go to them.

Alex spills out his feelings to Dave, whom he finds to be a sympathetic listener. Dave agrees that they will take the matter up at the first teachers meeting. Alex presses for having a number of matters settled then so that they need not be taken up again and teachers can devote themselves to teaching.

Dave and Alex are working at the second major item in preparing for the beginning of a year, the matter of the organization of a department.

The conflict of purposes between teaching and other matters is the result of what is called a sociological lag. Miss Gill, besides being a symbol of it, is an anachronism. The lag came about this way: the old Sunday school tradition stressed organization. Superintendents, assistant superintendents, secretaries for ordering, secretaries for attendance, secretaries for promotion, and so on, were persons who had important jobs to do in the organization. Attendance-keeping was a big thing because of the award system often used. Offering-taking was a big thing because the Sunday school took pride in supporting itself as a separate organization from the church. All this potentially good organization came to be top-heavy, somewhat like a lodge with its numerous functionaries.

Into this highly organized school there has come in the past few years a major reform in curriculum, a move toward regarding the school as the school of the church, and, above all, a heightened seriousness about the teaching task. Alex and Dave represent the new focus on teaching. When they begin to take it seriously they find much in the church school that defeats them.

As a matter of fact, Dave himself, if he were not of the new school of thought, might well be an anachronism. The department superintendent of the old school had a clearly defined job. He kept things organized, led the assembly or worship, supervised the other officers. In the well-run junior high department today there is little or no super-organization, no assembly or worship, the most unobtrusive kind of attendance-keeping, and no fanfare of offering-taking, especially if the junior highs attend the morning service of worship. The old job description of a department superintendent has disappeared. The new job description centers on teaching, and the superintendent is primarily the lead teacher for teachers. He works ahead of them, knowing the teaching materials and planning ways to help teachers do better work. It is this sort of thing that Dave is trying to do in setting up a teachers meeting (and what Dot does in stimulating Mary to read the next unit of study).

But, alas, few church schools are well run. Many teachers have difficulty teaching because the total schedule is set up for anything but teaching. It is planned for assembling, for so-called worship, for collecting attendance statistics and offerings, for handing out materials, for miscellaneous speakers and films, for promotional speeches by representatives of any churchwide program, for robing the youth choir, and so on. Though teachers may often feel helpless against such forces, the beginning of the year offers a good time to see if some of them cannot be done away with or mitigated.

As Alex did, they should press for an emphasis on teaching. They should ask how much time they will have and on which Sundays. They should consider together every interruption or extraneous matter that comes up during a Sunday morning. Are there other ways to accomplish these same things without breaking into classwork? They should raise questions about whole Sundays taken for other purposes. Are they necessary? Do they contribute to teaching? If teachers wish to be courageous about the matter, there are many ways to reduce and eliminate interruptions in a church school hour as well as Sundays preempted for other activities. They can also raise questions about assembling and "worshiping."

These organizational matters should be taken up as part of preparation for the year, settled, put into smooth operation, and, hopefully, not brought up again during the year. If later meetings of teachers are preoccupied with organizational matters, something is wrong with the organization.

If you teach in a yearly-theme system, look through your teaching materials for articles, outlines, and suggested resources that help you plan for the year ahead.

What other kinds of teachers meetings might be used for previewing subject matter?

How much sociological lag is there in your church school? Is there any conflict between a highly organized school and a strong teaching emphasis? If so, at what points does it show up? It is most likely to show up in the percentage of the total time that you have for classwork. For example, if you have only twenty minutes, something is wrong.

The weight of tradition, unthinkingly adopted, can be rather heavy, as you can see by discussing with other teachers: Why keep attendance records? Should there be an offering in Sunday church school?

Putting new wine into old wineskins is often so difficult that many workers with young adolescents would be well advised to start new kinds of programs outside the church school hour and tradition. For more about the possibility, see *The Young Adolescent in the Church*.

The matter of worship and the church school is taken up in *The Young Adolescent in the Church*, Chapter 2.

Planning Ahead for a Unit

Dot, who is in charge of the new Wednesday afternoon junior high program, purposely or accidentally reminds Mary that a new unit of study is coming up. She thus reminds Mary that she should be reading and planning ahead. Probably Dot intends to have a meeting of the adult workers at which they will make plans for the unit.

These two know that a unit is a group of related sessions. But the average teacher, especially the new teacher, is likely to bypass the unit as one of those newfangled things that make Sunday school more complicated than it should be.

Take Clarke, the new teacher who was introduced by means of a filmstrip to the view that the Bible tells one continued story. Clarke was being encouraged to take a long view of the year's work. When he begins to look at his curriculum materials he may well drop the long view. If he is an average teacher, he has behind him a long tradition of a lesson each Sunday (one reason the Saturday-night-glance type of preparation became possible). His own comments about the Bible being taught to him as stories and teachings show that he was taught this way.

Because of the filmstrip and the teachers meeting, Clarke may pay some attention to parts of his material that outline the year and the approach to be taken. Almost the next thing he comes across is a unit introduction. He skips over it because the whole thing does not make sense to him. He turns to the first session and tries to figure out what the lesson is, a matter that may not be altogether clear.

Suppose Clarke has been jogged out of the path of least resistance, which consists of teaching as he was taught. If he can look at the unit with an open mind, he will find that it gives him some valuable guidance in study with young adolescents (in contrast to the teaching-lessons approach).

For one thing, the unit will encourage him to take a broader approach to his background study than merely getting acquainted with what is coming up next Sunday. It will highlight for him the possibility of studying a larger block of background material. For example, in a certain unit, the junior highs are to study several portions of The Acts of the Apostles. When Clarke sees this he might well read the entire book as preparation. He could go on and study the passages to be taken up in classwork. Or perhaps he will do this later as he prepares for each session. In either case, the passages will already be in a larger framework for him, the framework of his acquaintance with the entire book. Probably in the long run, Clarke saves himself some time. More important is the fact that he has been helped at the point of his need for a larger framework of understanding.

As Clarke gets better acquainted with the way successive sessions relate to one another, he will see that he has some leeway in classwork. He does not need to be under pressure to bring each session to an absolute conclusion. Some things can carry over if not finished in one meeting. Certain activities, he sees, are designed to carry over from session to session throughout a unit.

However, Clarke is somewhat put off by the first unit he comes to. His resolution to be open-minded suffers a jolt. It would appear to be an introductory unit to the year of study. There are no Bible passages and no "lessons." Two or three sessions are taken for such matters as: recalling what the junior highs know, considering what they might learn or want to know, introducing the tools to be used, planning ways of working—all with the young people themselves having some say.

Clarke's view of teaching is the usual one of imparting information. Therefore, he thinks, why not plunge right in? Furthermore, the methods suggested for carrying out the purposes are completely strange to him. How can he carry on a discussion of what junior highs might learn or want to know? And why should he? He supposed the teaching material showed him what they ought to learn.

The introductory unit, with its peculiar methods, is showing Clarke how to be one who guides study, working alongside junior highs. As such he is to share with them a general introduction to the work ahead, help them set some of their goals and expectations, invite them to share in some of the planning. Above all, he is to demonstrate that their work is necessary and will be relied on.

What these add up to is an essential direction of work in which the junior highs are to be given as much responsibility for their own study as they can take. Clarke will use the same kind of approach and some of the same methods in the introductory session of each unit and at other times in classwork. The organization of material into units allows junior highs to take part in planning more frequently.

A glance at several units will show Clarke that they vary in length and in type, according to the subject matter. A unit of study in Old Testament material may be developed around an era of history. Such a division makes possible a clearer use of background material, since times and customs varied in the long span of time covered in the Old Testament.

A unit of study on the church may be similarly developed around a period of history, making it possible for the pupils to find out about the time and how people lived then.

In the study of Jesus Christ, a unit might be organized around a basic question of faith selected from the Bible material to be used and from the kinds of questions young people might ask. Or a unit might be planned around a period of time in the work of Jesus.

When Clarke plunges himself into the work of preparing for a unit, here are some of the things he will notice in a rapid preview:

—*generalities,* such as the purpose or general direction, the material (Bible or church history) to be taken up, how it relates to the junior highs as young Christians.

—*his own background study,* consisting of material provided in the teacher's manual, Bible passages, any material that the young people are to read. And in addition: other resources, books or parts of books for background study.

—*materials for class use,* including the session outlines that are the teacher's guide to classwork, any materials the pupils are to use such as notebook or reading book. And in addition: related picture sets, self-teaching devices, audio-visual aids; also books, pictures, magazines, or the like that may be available or borrowed for the use of the pupils.

After getting a quick overview of the unit, Clarke should set aside time for his own background *study* in which he can read the basic material to be taken up and any interpretive articles supplied in curriculum materials. At this point, he reads and thinks in terms of his own ideas, questions, and understandings. The initial part of study takes place in one sitting, when the teacher reads. The greater part of it takes place later and in odd moments, for example, while Adelaide is washing the dishes. Thus, the initial reading ought to be done as early as possible before going on to the next steps of unit preparation.

Clarke's next step should be to get acquainted with some of the *methods* to be used, the ways in which pupils and teacher will work together. To do so he should preview the session outlines by scanning them rapidly, perhaps stopping to read in more detail here and there. The introductory session and the last session, especially if it includes methods of review and reports from activities, should get special attention.

The new teacher needs to keep an open mind when he begins to select methods, as select he must. The time to make tentative selections is while the unit as a whole is being considered. Later, in the press of preparing for a session, the teacher is more likely to settle for teaching as he was taught. The proper bases on which he might make selection are the time and materials available, the known abilities or preferences of the class, and his own abilities. For example, a class of junior highs may think that informal dramatization is too childish for them. Perhaps the teacher who handles discussion with ease falls all over himself when it comes to supervising the work of planning an interview.

The improper bases of selection are the teacher's tendency to rely on what he knows and his fear to venture into new ways. The hesitant teacher has to dare himself to try new things rather than rely completely on what he knows he can do. Many teachers with strong preferences for tried and true ways project their preferences onto the junior highs. The teacher who claims that they want only discussion frequently means that he wants it.

Next Clarke should consider the suggested *activities* for the unit. Like many another teacher he will be tempted to bypass these as extras. For one thing, he will not think he has time to do them. For another, activities to him may call up shades of his primary days when the teacher passed out coloring sheets and crayons after the lesson. A closer look at his material will show Clarke that activities are the means by which junior highs find and use the background information essential in study. They are a part of study and contribute information used in classwork.

Here Clarke must make tentative choices again, for the class will not be able to carry out every one of the suggested activities. He may select one of several or decide that the pupils should select one. If the class is large, he may divide it into small groups to work out several activities. Perhaps he will plan with other teachers so that each class can choose one activity and the results of work can be shared.

Clarke's final step in unit preparation will be listing and locating materials needed, a bigger task than it seems when put into one sentence. Some of the materials will be books, pictures, audio-visual aids, all sources of information that will be on hand for the junior highs to use in classwork. Others will be supplies needed in carrying out activities, such as a large sheet of paper for making a poster in session 3.

This kind of unit preparation is a lot of work. But the time Clarke spends before the beginning of a unit will save him preparation time on each session. It will give him a larger framework of understanding of the material to be studied and greater ease in classwork. Because he has planned ahead, he will be better able to work with the junior highs as one who guides.

Look in your teaching materials for an example of a unit. (Materials that are not planned around an annual theme often have a definite unit organization.) What guidance is given the teacher for planning a unit? If none is given, how can you use the above ideas to make your own outline or chart of the unit? How is the unit introduced? In what ways do junior highs take part in the planning? Does the unit work toward a review or report session? What activities are suggested? In what ways are they part of the classwork?

Methods of planning with young adolescents are taken up in detail in Chapter 7.

Think about or discuss some differences between the lesson-each-Sunday approach and the unit approach. What advantages and disadvantages do you see in each?

Once you learn the unit approach, it will occur to you that it allows for many variations in teaching. For example, some units can be organized on a department-wide basis. Instead of each class covering all the sessions, each session plan can be assigned to a class. A full session at the end must be allowed for reporting so that all share in the results of the work.

Planning Ahead for a Session

THE TEACHER'S STUDY

In the episode at the beginning of the chapter, Adelaide has been reading a book about the church because it is the subject of study in the junior high class she teaches. With her hands in the dishwater, she thinks in an idle and typical (typical of everyone, that is) way about what she has read, relating it to her church, to the junior highs, to her own ideas. She is studying.

Irv, the night watchman, is reading the Bible passage that seventh graders in his class will explore in the next session. He brings imagination to his reading, by means of which he identifies himself with the prophet. He is concerned with himself and with what the Scripture says to him. For the moment, the junior highs he teaches are out of mind. He is studying.

The Super Company representative, Al, is reconstructing in his mind a time in church history. He has read the background information in his teacher's outlines and also some information supplied for the use of pupils in their notebook. He is thinking about the points of identification between young Christians today and people in the past. Soon he will turn to the Bible passages that the junior highs are to explore as if they were sixteenth-century Christians. He is studying.

The group of teachers of whom Thelma is one read and discuss the Bible passage they are to take up with junior highs. All of them have read it previously and have also read an interpretation of it that was given in their teaching materials. At this point, they are thinking of what questions the Bible material will raise in the minds of junior highs. They are doing so against the background of their study.

The camp counselor, Lucille, who is having to find her place again, is reading a part of the Bible that will be studied by junior high campers. She and the other counselors will consider what the passage says, the background of time and place for it, what it might say to junior highs, what they might ask of it. She is studying.

Ralph has come across a problem. He has learned that the New Testament letters were not essays, as he had once thought, but real letters written in answer to problems that churches were having in the early times. However, something in his teaching material had hinted that Ephesians was not that kind of letter. The junior highs in the current unit are making use of passages from Ephesians. Ralph has told them that Paul wrote the letter to the church at Ephesus but now he wonders whether that was correct. He is studying.

Vivian is reading in the newspaper about one of the most controversial issues today. Comments made by the junior highs in her class recall an incident from the Gospels they had been exploring. It included issues of law and law-abiding. In the understanding of these issues both Vivian and the junior highs had made only a tentative beginning. She is studying.

All these teachers are engaged in the first step of preparation, their own study. Ideally, the adult as a member of the church is one who studies. Practically speaking, he is most often prodded to do so by the responsibility he has undertaken toward young adolescents. Yet the teacher's initial study must be his own, focused on what he makes of the material studied, and not on what junior highs may do with it. (Even so, those young people are always flitting in and out of the picture.)

For this reason, some curriculum materials supply study articles apart from session outlines. Other materials guide the teacher to sources of information for study. In some cases, the main interpretation is embedded in the session plan. Other materials leave the teacher on his own when it comes to study.

The place to start is with the Bible passage or passages to be taken up in classwork (except in units on church history, in which the primary material is about Christians of other times). The way to approach it is with the expectation that it will say something new.

Next the study-er turns to any interpretation of it, whether in a study article supplied in the teacher's materials or in outside resources. The order of these two can be reversed, but probably the order suggested here is better. The study-er will many times want to turn to the Bible passage again after he has read an interpretation of it.

There may be other resources, such as the kind Ralph is looking for, that the teacher will want to consult for historical or other background information. Sometimes such information is supplied for him or supplied for the young people in their materials. Directions for the junior highs' fact-finding work will often show the teacher where to look for background information.

The wise teacher will do this much as early as possible, so that he has time to "Oh! H'm. I see! Yes, but" over it. In a Sunday-to-Sunday schedule, for example, the reading should be done at the latest on Sunday evening for the following Sunday's session. Better still, of course, would be broader study in preparation for the unit, so that study for any one session is mostly review.

The teacher's study is a means by which he stirs himself to think, consider, and weigh on his own level of understanding. The insights he comes to will be adult ones, dependent on experiences young adolescents have not had. What the teacher takes to classwork from his own study consists not of his conclusions but of a larger framework of understanding.

Neither the study material itself nor the teacher's thoughts are "the lesson" to be taught. If they were, the teacher's work would be mostly done at this point. He would need only to devise some ways of putting the lesson across or applying it to the pupils. Instead, he is to guide young adolescents toward their own insights in the study of the same material.

PLANS FOR CLASSWORK

The next question and step for the teacher who has studied is, How will adult and young adolescents work together in studying the same material? In the episodes at the beginning of the chapter, Al, Thelma, Irene, Sandra, Lyall, Vivian, Ralph, and Brad are all engaged in various parts of this step.

Al, taking a flight of fancy out of Flight 608, goes back to the sixteenth century with his junior highs to take a look around. Actually, he is thinking no farther than the next Sunday. He is planning how the young people can identify themselves with Christians of another time. He has a definite method, the acting out of a secret cottage meeting, to consider. His thoughts indicate that there may be ample ground for identification.

Thelma and her fellow workers are planning the schedule for Sunday's session, as they do every week. They plan in terms of a large group of junior highs broken into varying small groups, instead of for individual classes. They are setting up new groups of junior highs to do fact-finding work for the unit. One of the groups, the one Thelma is to work with, is to report during the session. The report is to be followed by small groups for Bible-reading and discussion. The teachers are trying out different questions that might be taken up.

Irene is getting acquainted with a teaching aid she plans to use, several frames of a filmstrip. The frames and the script will give the junior highs information as well as help them visualize the people and the time of the Bible material to be studied. Irene previews the audio-visual aid in order to see what the junior highs might learn from it. She plans a way to introduce the frames and ways to use the information from them for further discussion. In addition, she makes arrangements for smooth and unobtrusive projection of the filmstrip.

Sandra is working with a group of junior highs who have been asked to prepare a dramatization to present in class. They are trying spontaneous dramatization of what they want to show. Sandra feels that the junior highs must know more about what they are acting out so that the presentation can be of help to those who will watch it. The dramatization will be a way of helping both actors and audience live into a happening in New Testament times. It may follow work with the Bible passages on which it is based or such work may be done after the dramatization.

Lyall is preparing a simple teaching aid to be used in

class work. His word list will help the junior highs read the Bible with greater understanding.

Vivian is collecting material from current sources that may help ninth graders think more deeply about issues raised in considering a Bible passage. In the light of past discussions, Vivian is fairly sure the issue will come up again. If so, she will have on hand the two clippings with their opposite points of view. From them she might read key sentences or ideas to help the ninth graders discuss further.

Ralph is seeking a piece of information for his own understanding. He may also use it in classwork if what he learns shows that he misinformed the junior highs. Ralph is supplying factual information that will help the young people understand the book of Ephesians better through knowing about its origin and considering what it meant to the people to whom it was addressed.

Brad, who seems to be looking backward, is also looking forward to the next session. He is recalling to himself what the junior highs thought and what reactions they had in previous study. His notes may not indicate what the young people will think at another time. But they give him information about his own pupils that he will use in adapting the curriculum suggestions for his class.

Planning for classwork starts when the teacher reads the session plan in his teaching material to get an overall view. None of the teachers described here started "cold" from his own study to figure out what the junior highs would do in study. The different ideas for methods, schedule, activities, committee work, teaching aids, discussion questions—all came from session outlines. The teachers, in planning ahead, are trying such ideas out for size.

Session or teaching plans are suggestions for the work that might be undertaken by adult and young adolescents together. To be sure, they can be approached in different ways. One teacher, the one who is still looking for a lesson to get over, will take them as what *he* must do. His picture of classwork is himself doing things. Another teacher will take the suggestions in a session plan as what he *must* do. Yet most session outlines offer a variety of methods and approaches among which the teacher must make choices. Many teachers think that the session plan is their teaching plan. Usually, however, the outline in curriculum material is not intended to be what the teacher will have at hand during class time. It is intended as a guide to the teacher's work of preparation, to be used at home and left at home. What the teacher takes to class is his own teaching plan, the result of his work with the printed session outline.

After getting acquainted with all the possibilities suggested to him in the session plan, the teacher engages in a process of putting himself in the place of his pupils (what Al is doing). What will they do in study? is the essential question. The question of what the teacher will do is, in a way, a secondary one. He will guide and supervise the things junior highs will do.

Other questions the teacher explores are: What understandings might the junior highs bring to such work? What particular points may relate to their thoughts? What possible insights and conclusions might they come to? (Thelma and her fellow teachers are taking up such questions.) Answers to some of these questions are suggested in the session plan.

To them must be added what the teacher knows about the young adolescents in his class, specific knowledge that only he has (like the things Brad recalls as he reads over his notes). Out of such knowledge and some knowledgeable hunches, not out of a general knowledge of adolescents and, above all, not out of his own preferences, the teacher selects among the possible procedures. He adapts, elaborates, and condenses the suggestions to fit his class and the time and resources available to him.

After he has considered what the junior highs will do, and possibly say and think, then the teacher decides how he will introduce and supervise the work. He continues to imagine the class at work until he has in mind a step-by-step procedure, with some alternate possibilities tucked away in case they are needed (such as the schedule worked out by Thelma and the other teachers in her department).

There is always an "if" in planning for any session. The "if" is, if things go as the teacher has planned. They may not because the classwork is essentially what the junior highs do. Discussion may take an unexpected turn. A suggested procedure may merely leave the young people saying, "So what?" A piece of work may take longer than the teacher has planned. The pupils may suggest another way of working better than the one the teacher had in mind. The more alternate possibilities the teacher has considered, even if they are ones he more or less discarded, the better prepared he is to work with young people. In other words, he must be overprepared. This is one reason materials always supply more suggestions than the teacher can use.

At this point the teacher is ready to make a written plan for himself. Some teachers use a notebook, in which they write their teaching plans. Others put notes on small cards or slips of paper. Skilled teachers work from memory, without any written plan at hand. Probably every teacher ought to make it his aim to become that skilled.

The teacher's final step in preparation will be locating and assembling the things needed for the session. Like Irene, he may need to preview an audio-visual aid. Like Lyall, he may prepare his own teaching aid. Like Vivian, he may have filed away some clippings that could be used in discussion. Locating needed materials may mean going to the library to borrow books or checking on whether there is chalk to use on the chalkboard. In the teacher's plan, making a list on the chalkboard can seem a good thing to do at a certain point. It may turn out to be not so good if the teacher suddenly discovers there is no chalk or has to send a junior high out to find some.

As after-class work, the teacher should make notes of what was done and said. The notes should be as complete as possible (like the ones Brad jotted down in the margins of his teaching material). Such notes will be a useful reminder of what the pupils are thinking. They can also remind the teacher that the work of the class is shared work. If his notes are more full of what he said and did than of what the junior highs said and did, he is probably tending to become a fount of knowledge rather than one who guides study.

Why are the teacher's study and planning for classwork two separate steps in preparing for a session?

Look through your teaching materials for suggestions of what the teacher should study.

Take a good look at a session outline. What different methods of work are suggested? What kind of schedule is suggested? What guidance is given about understandings junior highs may bring to the work, and insights they might gain? What materials are needed for teaching? What differences are there between a session that is a performance by the teacher and one in which the emphasis is on the work the junior highs do?

Before going on to the next chapters, which give more detailed information about methods, go through this chapter again quickly. Underline or put a check mark alongside the methods of class work hinted at here and there with which you are not familiar. In other words, put a mark wherever in reading you said to yourself, "What does that mean?"

7. Planning

How can the adult help young adolescents take responsibility for their own study?

Two Extremes

The first and most important answer to this recurring question lies in the structure of program for young adolescents. It should be a structure based on the understanding that no one is going to, and, indeed, no one can, give young people anything except guidance in their own work. A second answer, the one that concerns the teacher more immediately, is that classwork includes having junior highs take part in planning their own work.

One teacher will think that "planning their own work" means gathering a group of junior highs and asking, "What do you want to do?" His idea is more or less in line with a recent, but well-entrenched, trend in youth work in the church.

A moment's reflection shows the impossibility of such an open-ended approach. The material for study, the story of faith, is not something that can be discovered in the interests, needs, or experiences of the young people. It comes to them from the outside, and the teacher's responsibility is to bring together the something from the outside and the inside of young lives. From a practical point of view, anyone who has tried it knows that asking young people what they want to do is futile. They seldom know or, at least, can seldom say.

Another teacher, having thought the matter through to this point, will retreat to the opposite extreme and ally himself with a much older tradition in church teaching. It is enough, he thinks, to announce the subject of study and start to work. If the subject is already decided on, why fool around or deceive the kids with thinking they have anything to do with the choice?

The question is a good one. It would be even better if study involved a solid block of information to pass on and measurable compartments in junior high minds in which to deposit it. In that case, the teacher would be merely a conveyer.

But study takes into account the responsibility of the young person for his own involvement with Scripture, which suggests there must be a middle ground between the extremes of "What do you want to do?" and "Do this! Do that!"

What comes to your mind when it is said that junior highs should take part in planning their own work?

How would you define the middle ground between the two extremes suggested here?

In order to find some middle ground, you are invited to guide an imaginary opening session of a unit. The greater amount of planning takes place in such a session, although there are other kinds of planning in other sessions. The unit is on the medieval era in church history.

"We" in the following and in similar sections of the next chapters, means, "we, the teacher."

Assuming that we have done the kind of unit preparation outlined in Chapter 6, and have planned the first session, in order to carry out our plans we shall—

Start with the Meeting Place

(Our class has a room of its own, which is the best kind of meeting place if space allows for it. Some adaptations to other meeting places are suggested in the section "Some Questions and / or Complaints.")

Our aim is to make the room a study center on Christians in the Middle Ages.

First we take a look around at the room. Let's remove everything that does not have to do with the work of the coming unit. If we are not accustomed to using our space as a study center, there may be considerable flotsam and jetsam to take away, including unused hymnbooks, old magazines, dog-eared copies of the pupils' notebooks, a map of Palestine, a 1940 calendar with a religious picture, mottoes, attendance charts for 1913, the Sunday school banner from 1890, the cradle roll, a mural made by the third grade three years ago, and dust. Or, if the room is used primarily for another activity, such as cooking or women's association meetings, we may need to provide ways to conceal or at least to focus attention away from such functions to that of study.

If we have used the room well in a previous unit, we remove the things that pertain only to our work then. We no longer need material about Christians in the first century, for example. Some things we want to keep. One is a time line we use almost every week in order to keep before us a view of what happened when. Another might be a list of questions to explore this year, which the class made out in the first sessions of the fall quarter.

Into a more or less bare room we bring all the things we have gathered for the unit that is about to begin. Our gatherings include some pictures from old copies of *Life* and *National Geographic,* a set of postcard-sized pictures ordered from a museum, a picture of a knight in armor, a list of books about medieval times that we found in the youth room of the local library, and other items. Yes, we have a suitcaseful, and we find that is the best way to get everything here.

With these, we—

Arrange a Display

Maybe we have a built-in bulletin board to use or can borrow one to stand on an easel. Perhaps we have to use the wall (taking care to use nonmarking materials to fasten pictures to it). We group several of the pictures to show various aspects of medieval life—for example, a castle, a cathedral, a picture of the inside of a cathedral, several pictures of such people as serfs, knights, ladies, and church officials.

Then we—

Add a Question

We shall do this especially if the pupils are not accustomed to looking at a display—for example, if it is the first time we have planned one. On a piece of drawing paper or cardboard, we write (legibly with felt-tip pen so that the lines are heavy and visible from a distance), "What was it like to be a member of the church in the Middle Ages?" We put our sign in a central place among the pictures.

Instead of this question, or in addition to it, we might write out a suggestion for each pupil and plan to hand out the slips of paper when they arrive. A sample suggestion would be: "Find out [or, "Be ready to tell"] one fact about the way people dressed [or about their houses, or churches, or about the classes of people] in the Middle Ages."

In addition to the display and a question, we—

Arrange Other Sources of Information

Along with our gatherings of pictures, we have collected a number of books and other materials that the junior highs can use in finding out about medieval times. Perhaps our room has an extra table of small size on which we can arrange these. If not, we may put them down the center of our worktable. Later we might arrange them as a small library on the windowsill, on a bookcase, or on a shelf.

Among these resources are other pictures and articles from magazines, some books borrowed from the church library or the public library (or a list of those available if they could not be borrowed), perhaps a filmstrip and projector if the junior highs can use it on their own, charts, a map, a copy of the pupils' reading book with chapters marked by colored plastic paper clips, the rest of the post-card-sized pictures not used in the display.

It occurs to us that it would be a good idea to copy the question at the center of the display and put it among the books and pictures. The question can give junior highs a reason for looking at these also.

We step back to take a look at the study center we have arranged. What have we provided up to this point? An *announcement* of a new subject of study, without relying solely on the teacher's verbal announcement. A *focusing* on the central purpose of the unit (in the question used with the display). *Materials* that invite the junior highs to find out for themselves. A *place* for work.

All this we have done long before—

The Junior Highs Arrive

Because we have provided materials and made them available and attractive beforehand, we allow time for the pupils to look around when they come to class. There are several ways to make use of the looking around. Finding answers to the question is one, or carrying out suggestions made to individual members of the class. We might speak to each pupil, pointing out the question in the display, asking him to look around and decide on some answers to it that he will later share with the class (not primarily with the teacher). We might ask each one, in relation to the display, whether he has studied medieval times in school, and if so, when and how.

The looking-around time need not be long, and we gather the pupils into one group for—

Conversation About What We Know

What the junior highs know at this point may be only what they have found in looking around the room. We ask each pupil to answer the question he was given, if we passed out individual questions or suggestions. Or we spend a few minutes talking over possible answers to the question in the display.

What the junior highs know may include much that they have learned in school. Their learning may be recent or it may date back a couple of years. One of the chief reasons for finding out what junior highs know is to locate and make use of general knowledge. It is especially necessary to do so in studies on the church, in which much background material overlaps with general history. We take time, therefore, to have several members of the class recall things they have learned, read, heard, and seen on TV or in the movies. There is no reason at this time for us to correct what seem to be mistaken ideas, although the junior highs may correct each other when such ideas are expressed.

We may find yet another strand among the things young adolescents already know that stems from work they have done previously in the church. Because of the nature and structure of church school work, certain subjects may be taken up again several times. Perhaps the fact is not so much of a problem in the unit we are starting. It can be seen clearly as a problem when junior highs approach a study of Jesus Christ. Many young people react against having to "do it all over again." They have such a reaction especially if teachers believe that the subject is a block of material to be mastered by repetition every few years. What junior highs need is assurance that they are not going to be drilled in the same old stuff. They are going to look at the basic sources of information again, and these do not change. But they will be looking at them from a different point of view because they themselves are different.

Sometimes it is necessary to bring out into the open an implied complaint, "Why do we go over this again?" and talk it over. If so, we must be ready to listen to a number of complaints and to refrain from combating them directly. In fact, we had better not say anything. When given a chance to say what they feel, most junior highs begin, on their own, to see some reasons for restudying a subject. It may still be important to reassure them that they are not going to approach it as children. The fact can be demonstrated by asking them to recall what they thought when they were children, and contrasting it with what they now think.

However, in the case of the unit on the Middle Ages, all this may not be necessary. It may be sufficient for us to point the way ahead by focusing on—

The Central Question

Next we turn to the question that we placed in the midst of the display: "What do you think it was like to be a member of the church in the Middle Ages?" We make a slight variation in it and emphasize "member of the church" a little. At this point we are moving away from background information toward the focus of thought and discussion in the unit. We allow time for a number of suggestions from the group, perhaps calling on a few of those to whom we talked in the opening minutes of the session. Answers will be more or less uninformed, or slightly informed from the looking-around time, or informed by recall from church school work at the junior level. We are still interested only in locating the information and ideas the pupils have, so we are not concerned to arrive at any special answers. But we are listening with an "extra ear" for clues that will help us refine our plans for the unit ahead.

Now the group needs a change of pace, which we get as we take up the question—

How Can We Find Out?

At this time we allow a few minutes for the junior highs to look over the tools they will be using and to search for ways to work. Perhaps at the beginning of the year, we had to show each piece of material and tell about it. By midyear the pupils should have gained some acquaintance with their tools and be able to look them over on their own. Their tools are the following:

—reading matter supplied for junior highs, primarily for reading at home.

—Bible material (in the unit we are planning it is not the primary source material and is used only at the end of the unit in order to help junior highs identify themselves with people who did not have access to the Bible).

—notebook plans for session-by-session use, including background information and ideas for procedures.

—suggestions or work outlines for fact-finding activities.

—assignments for outside work and/or devotional materials, if provided.

—other resources, curriculum-related (pictures and audio-visual aids), or additional materials (books from library, clippings, and the like).

Perhaps we let the pupils search for ideas among these things haphazardly, sending them to the book table and the display to look at what is available. Perhaps, instead, we ask individual pupils or committees of two to examine specific items and to bring back ideas to the class. One pupil or a committee will preview for the others what the pupils are to read for the unit. Another will put before the class several possible activities for getting more background information. Still another might preview things that individual pupils could do outside of class time.

What we are doing here is helping the pupils see how they can work on their own, in committees, in the full class group, outside of class time. They will have to make decisions about: What shall we do? Who will do it? How shall we do it?

From a general view of the work ahead, we turn to consider the suggested activities in more detail. Very likely, choices are necessary among the fact-finding activities, a possibility we have anticipated in our advance planning. Perhaps the entire class will work on one of them. It would be better, however, to divide all or some of them among individual pupils or small committees. The junior highs themselves may come up with different suggestions. Suppose, for example, in addition to finding information and sharing it for class use, some of them want to use it also to prepare living pictures of medieval people in costume and have a narrator to explain the pictures. It is a possibility we had not planned for, but we add it to the other suggestions being considered.

The following are some matters we talk over in deciding what to do:

Time. Can we carry this out in class time? and/or with additional individual work at home? and/or with extra meetings?

People. Are there enough of us to do the necessary work?

Resources. Can we find out enough facts from what we have or can find in our community, in books, films, filmstrips, and pictures, people who are experts?

Contribution to classwork. Will it help us with our central question or take us off on a tangent?

The next step is deciding who will do what. Perhaps we let those who have a preference choose what they wish to do. Some work, we remember, can be carried out by an individual pupil just as well as by a group. For example, perhaps only one pupil wants to find out about church buildings. If so, we need not insist that several pupils work on the activity. Sometimes we prefer to divide the class arbitrarily into small committees and assign an activity to each. We might do this especially when, on the basis of choice, certain pupils have always worked together and we wish to make new groupings.

To take up the question of how to do the work, we allow each work group or committee time to meet, to look over or plan an outline for its work, to decide on first steps, and to look ahead to how its work will be shared with others in the class. We spend time with each group or individual, getting the work started, making suggestions of resources and methods, and the like.

(If we are new to ways of letting junior highs take responsibility for their own work, we may emphasize the fact-finding activities, even considering them the only things that the pupils can do on their own and contribute to classwork. As we learn how to work alongside young adolescents with greater ease we shall find that more and more of the planning and work become theirs.)

After planning ways to work, we may have time in the session to do another kind of planning by—

Raising Questions

In the context of the background information we plan to develop, we return to our central question, rephrasing it to, "What would you like to know about being members of the church in the Middle Ages?"

By now the junior highs have more sense of where their explorations might go. We allow time for them to suggest *questions the class might explore,* and we list them on chalkboard or paper under such a heading. If the class listed some general questions at the beginning of the year, we refer to them also.

While ideas are expressed we keep the central question before the junior highs as a criterion for accepting suggestions that are to the point and rejecting or redirecting those that are not to the point. For example, someone may want to know whether it was true that priests controlled everything and told people what to do. Such a question is to the point and goes on our list.

Another junior high may want to know more about how wars were fought. That kind of question we might refer to one of the fact-finding committees or ask the pupil himself to find out and tell the rest of us. The questions in our list are about what it meant to be members of the church— how faith was learned and expressed. Faith may have been and in this case was expressed in war, so wanting to know about war is not entirely irrelevant. We might recast the pupil's question to, "Why did Christians go to war as an expression of their faith?" Such a question will lead us into thinking about, considering, and weighing factual information. And it is this kind of direction we wish to set in raising questions.

We take the list of questions home or copy it from the chalkboard. The junior highs' ideas will be useful to us in going over our plans for the unit. From the list we choose the more important or most frequently recurring questions and those which it will be possible to explore. We write or print them on a large piece of paper or poster board. The poster goes to class with us next time. We put it with the display or somewhere else in the room to remind the junior highs of the direction their work will take.

Now let us look back to see what we have done. We have:

—set before the junior highs a new area of exploration.

—invited them to get acquainted with its possibilities.

—helped them recall their own knowledge (or, maybe, ignorance) of it.

—let the young people get acquainted with tools and consider how they might use them.

—decided together what background information may be needed and how to get it.

—planned some ways to acquire and to share background information.

—given tentative direction to our work by hearing some of the young people's questions about the central purpose.

—perhaps disarmed the complaint of the "same old stuff" and helped the group make a new approach.

—and, most important of all, established a way of working and an atmosphere that say: "You can do this. It is your work to do."

Before reading further, go through this section again. Mark or make lists of ideas that are new to you (√), suggestions that seem strange to you (?), and those which seem impossible to you (X).

Look back to the section "Planning Ahead for a Unit" in Chapter 6. Where and how do the steps of preparation show up in the steps of introducing a unit? For example, why were "we" able to redirect a question for information about war toward the question of war as an expression of faith?

VARIATIONS

The first session of a unit with its introductory and planning work will usually include the steps outlined here. The methods by which the steps are developed may vary, however. Here are some other methods divided according to the basic steps.

Questions we want to explore. A question box can be added to the display, with paper and pencil available so that junior highs can write their questions. "What do you want to know about the Bible?" "What are your questions about Jesus Christ?" "What would you like to know about being a member of the church?"—these are general questions that will stimulate thought. Junior highs have some ideas about them. Such questions as: "What do you want to know about being members of the church in the Middle Ages?" or, "What do you want to know about the time of the prophets?" would probably be premature if asked at the very beginning of acquaintance with a new subject of study. The junior highs would not yet have enough information to know what questions they want to ask. One or two pupils can go over the questions quickly and report to the others on what members of the class (in general, not by name) would like to know. Or the teacher can do this, catching a few moments to go over the questions while the pupils are at work on something else. The report may need to be held over until the next session.

What we now know or think. Thought questions, to which junior highs write individual answers, will often bring out ideas. "Why study the Bible?" "I think the reformation of the church started by Luther was important because . . ." "Jesus Christ is important to me because . . ." "If I could go back in time and talk to one of the apostles in the early church, I would ask him . . ." "The church is . . ." These are the kinds of questions that might be asked. If the teacher gives a report to the class about the answers, it should be made in terms of "what we now think." He may not give a report; he may use the questions to inform his own planning. Or he may put the answers away and have the pupils reread them after several sessions or even units, to see if they still agree with their earlier ideas.

What we think and *Questions we want to explore.* An opinion survey or quiz may also locate present ideas and understandings. Several opinions of the church might be suggested to find out which junior highs agree with. They might be asked to consider different interpretations of Jesus Christ, perhaps by looking at a number of pictures or by considering how people think about him. A game of rapid association to words can be used also. For example, the teacher asks, "What do you think of when I say 'Christian'?" Answers should be the first thing that comes to mind. Part of the purpose here is to confront young people with the fact that there are many differing ideas and interpretations in order to help them approach a subject thoughtfully and to raise questions of their own.

What we need to know. Sometimes the first session of a unit begins by immediate involvement with the source material. For example, study of the rescue of the people under Moses might be the first step in a unit about the forming of God's people. A unit on Christians in the second century might start with taking part in their kind of meeting. In both cases, the actions studied are central and determinative for the times. The forming of God's people began in and was wholly determined by their rescue by God. Much of the life of Christians in early times centered around their worship. From consideration of these central events the junior highs can turn to the kinds of information needed (fact-finding activities), the questions they wish to explore, and the tools available to them.

What we need to know. There is another way in which the need for information-finding activities might be developed as source material is studied. Suppose, for example, that junior highs begin to read in the Gospel of John. The problems they encounter in reading can lead to planning the work ahead. It will soon be evident that they must find out the meanings of words. The need for background information will be clear and urgent. Some may sense the need for knowing more about the Gospel itself, when it was written, and why. All these needs can be expanded into fact-finding activities that will aid in classwork.

A look ahead. A filmstrip or portion of a filmstrip showing some of the main events of the time to be studied is one of the best ways to help junior highs get information that will aid them in planning ahead. A great deal depends on how the teacher views and uses such an audio-visual aid, however. It can't be shown to the class without introduction and discussion, or with the idea that, once the young people have seen this, they know all there is to know. Therefore, the central question, or a variation of it, is used to introduce the visualization. In the unit on the Middle Ages the junior highs would be asked to look for clues to what it was like to be members of the church then. Follow-up discussion might start with this question. The facts given in the filmstrip will be beginning points for further exploration. Discussion after seeing the filmstrip will include such comments as: "We saw that monasteries were an important part of the church in medieval times. How can we find out more about them and their importance?"

Questions we want to explore. A previously given assignment might be the starting point for considering the work ahead. For example before a unit centering on the reactions of various people to Jesus Christ, junior highs might be asked to skim their own background reading material or, say, the Gospel of Mark, looking for different people who met Jesus and how they reacted to him. Before a unit about the beginnings of the church, they might ask a number of their acquaintances what they think the church is or why the church is important. Both of these assignments can lead to seeing a variety of ideas, thus helping junior highs think about what they want to know.

A look ahead. A time line and map are essential items in looking ahead to most units. They can be used rapidly for suggesting when and where things took place, but they should be in view throughout the unit.

What we now know. At times it is helpful to construct with the pupils a time line for a period of time they know about from their schoolwork. For example, in finding out about Christians in early America, the junior highs might try to reconstruct what they recall about the time. Events, rather than dates, should be emphasized, but some attempt should be made to put them in order. A similar procedure can be used in study of Jesus Christ. Junior highs can be asked to recall events in the life of Christ. They need not attempt to put them in order (which is uncertain because of variations in the Gospels), but they might see how much they remember. In a study of Old Testament times, the technique can be used to review and to put a coming unit in the larger picture. Rather than asking junior highs to recall on their own, the teacher might supply slips of paper with names and events, and ask the pupils to put them in approximate order to show the history of God's people.

Why is it important to establish a way of working and an atmosphere that invite young adolescents to do their own work? If you are not sure, reread Chapter 3.

Why is it necessary to give so much attention to background information? If you are not sure, turn back to the section "Time and Place" in Chapter 4.

Why should there be a unit on Christians in the Middle

Ages? If you are not clear about this, reread Chapter 5, especially the section "The People of God and the World."

Look through your own teaching materials for sessions in which new units are introduced. What methods are suggested for helping junior highs plan their own work?

The development and use of fact-finding activities are taken up in the next chapter.

SOME QUESTIONS AND/OR COMPLAINTS

While "we" have been demonstrating how junior highs take part in planning their own work, other teachers have been crowding forward with questions, some of which sound like complaints.

"That's all very well, but we don't have a room," says one teacher. Provided the class meets in part of a room that can be somewhat screened off from other classes, the teacher can do all the things suggested here. Even if the room is undivided, with classes meeting in different corners, there is no reason the suggested procedures cannot be followed. Once junior highs are absorbed in work they are not much aware of other classes at work around them. (The problem is entirely different if they are supposed to be absorbed only in listening.)

Suppose, however, the class meets in a pew or in so small a room that there is space only for a table and chairs. By using some ingenuity, the teacher in such a situation can still carry out all the kinds of work suggested.

Instead of having a bulletin board for the display, he can use the nearest wall or he can prop a large piece of cardboard (the side of a box, such as a furniture or appliance carton) against the wall. If neither of these is possible, he can make a two-part bulletin board to hang over the back of the pew in front of the pupils. (It requires two pieces of heavy cardboard or wallboard joined by two strings so that the boards balance each other. The height at which the board hangs should be checked. It should hang as near the eye level of seated pupils as possible, and the strings should be adjusted accordingly.)

Since space for pictures may be limited, the question might be omitted. Instead, the teacher could make a copy of it to pass out to each pupil. The question will be better used if it also includes something specific for the pupil to find out—a combination of the question and the suggestion.

Books, extra pictures, and other resources can be laid out on the pew itself so that the junior highs cannot sit down without taking them up. Or the teacher can arrange books in a lightweight suitcase placed in the center of the pew. A makeshift bookshelf can be made by cutting down a cardboard carton so that books stand up in it. The shelf can be placed on the pew. Pictures and clippings can be put in several large envelopes according to subject divisions. Several envelopes are better than one, so that no pupil has to wait for someone else to finish looking through all of them to find what he wants.

When the pupils arrive, they cannot look at materials by walking around. But if materials are centrally placed, they can be within reach of any member of the class. The teacher's job is to encourage pupils to reach. He does this best by giving each one a question to look up. He may even put the question slips in the books or attach them to pictures and clippings, and hand out a piece of material to each pupil. This would be a method to use only when the teacher is introducing the idea of junior highs looking up information. Later when they know where and how to look on their own, they will consider that they are being treated as children if things are handed to them.

In dividing into committees or small groups, the teacher's best procedure is to make groups according to the seating arrangement in order to avoid moving about (although it is not impossible for several members of the class to shift places). Three in a row or two next to each other can get their heads together to plan and work. Two or three groups of junior highs talking among themselves actually make little more noise than one teacher talking to a class.

To have a place for listing questions, the teacher can make a blank turnover chart by thumbtacking several pieces of shelf paper or newsprint to a piece of wallboard. Writing should be done with a felt-tip pen or marking crayon. The board can be propped in the lap for writing and held up before the class when the list is completed. Once a sheet of paper has been used, it can be flipped back over the top of the board or torn off.

Sometimes the work of recording questions is done by a member of the class, perhaps on a clipboard. He writes down the questions with pencil and paper and reads them to the class later, instead of having them in a form that all can see.

"I don't have that much time," comes the voice of another teacher. He may be complaining about the changed role of the teacher. He means to say, "I don't have time to do all these things and teach the lesson too." Work of the kind outlined here takes away from the teacher a certain kind of initiative and places it squarely in front of the pupils, where it belongs. The teacher has a new kind of initiative to take and changed responsibilities that may well seem new and strange. The young people are invited to explore, rather than to hear. The teacher is the one who lays before the pupils the possibilities, the tools, the methods for their work. He uses his greater store of information about the subject, not as something to stuff into young minds, but as that which can stimulate and inform their work of exploring. He also has an accumulated knowledge of methods and resources that he makes available to the pupils. This is altogether a different stance for the teacher to take; it requires some time to learn. The best method of learning, however, is doing.

Perhaps the complainer about time means that he has only twenty minutes for classwork, and he rightly sees that he cannot do all those things in twenty minutes. There are no practical adaptations to suggest for a shortage of time as there are for a shortage of space. The problem is not one of trying to cut everything down to fit into a few minutes. The problem is how to get more class time. Teachers who begin to take seriously the possibility of study with young adolescents begin to itch for more time. They should take the itch seriously. Doing something about the matter may require going deeper than the question of interruptions raised in Chapter 6. It may mean meeting with the committee on Christian education to consider the entire program for junior highs, and whether and how it can provide time for study.

"I don't have all those extra materials," says another teacher. Many a teacher is put off when he sees a list of outside resources that might be used in a unit. Overwhelmed by what he doesn't have, he fails to see what he does have or can get. He has, usually, many resources within the teaching materials themselves. However, he is accustomed to thinking of them as "things to get across"—surely too many—rather than resources the junior highs can use in developing their own work. If the teacher will get more acquainted with the things supplied and consider them from the point of view of study, he will find they take on a different aspect. Then, it is seen, there are really too few of them.

Even though the teacher sees that outside resources are valuable and necessary, he is often offended by the length of the list. He tends to think, "I can't have all of these, so I haven't anything." Most lists of outside resources are long because they include alternate suggestions. No one needs to have everything, but almost everyone can have some things.

Gathering outside materials, such as pictures and clippings, is a matter of planning ahead. It is a well-known fact of life that, if you read or hear a new word—say, "salpiglossis"—one day, you are almost certain to come across "salpiglossis" again in a few days. In fact, it seems to turn up everywhere. The same thing happens to the prepared teacher. Somewhere in his advance study he comes across the name "Megiddo," a town associated with King Solomon. Like magic, the newspaper carries an article about archaeological finds at Megiddo. He might have overlooked the article except that he had been alerted to the name Megiddo. Good teachers are good gatherers. Good gatherers are those who have been alerted by a wide acquaintance with the subject matter of study.

Sometimes the gathering can be delegated to someone else. A junior high department might ask a person who is not a teacher to study the teaching materials ahead, search for clippings, pictures, and the like, mount them, file them, and supply the teachers with a list. The job is a challenging one. It requires a good reader who likes to deal with facts. Almost every church has someone, a housewife or retired person, who would enjoy that type of work.

When it comes to purchasing materials, the place to start, is, obviously, with the less-expensive items on the list. Perhaps a few of them will be sufficient, or a few of them along with borrowed books.

The first place in which to look for books to borrow is the church library, if there is one. Many church librarians make it a point to keep abreast of teaching materials. They regularly select and order books which they think would be useful. They usually welcome suggestions from teachers. Some librarians supply teachers with lists of books related to the subject of study. Most church libraries are waiting to be discovered by both teachers and pupils. Others are waiting to be started through the efforts of teachers who make known their need for outside resources.

The second place in which to look is the public library. It is better to inquire at the public library for the exact books needed, or, at least, to ask for books on a certain subject, such as Old Testament times or the Roman Empire. It would be a mistake to ask the librarian simply for "religious books" or "Bible-story books." Sometimes books can be borrowed on the teacher's card or by special arrangement for class use. If not, the teacher can make a list of those available. Or some junior highs can be sent to the library to make a list, after the teacher has been there first to find out whether any books are available. Some reference books that junior highs can use will be found in adult sections rather than in youth rooms. (In some states, it is possible to borrow from a central library books that are not available in the local library. This is a possibility to investigate also.)

Church budgets for Christian education should include amounts for buying books and other materials. Many times they do, but the teacher never knows this unless he inquires whether it would be possible to purchase each year a few books to use in the junior high department. Sometimes the inquiry starts people thinking that it might be possible. All else failing, probably the thing to do is to find a wealthy patron who would like to donate a sum of money to buy books, or a large group of parents who would give fifty cents apiece to start a library.

There are a few other possibilities that ought not to be overlooked. If junior highs are accustomed to working with many resources, and most of them are, they can find sources of information to use outside class time or to bring to class. They may have access to school libraries, which usually the teacher will not have. There are always encyclopedias available in libraries, schools, and many homes.

Even if outside resources are more available than it seems at first glance, there are still some problems in using them. What happens, for example, if a church owns one Bible dictionary, and six junior high classes are supposed to use it, not to mention a senior high class? One possibility is to keep the dictionary in the library and send students to it as necessary. Most teachers would think such a thing impossible, even though junior highs do it every day in school. For one thing, think of the valuable time lost while a pupil goes to the library—which means, all that time in which nothing is said. It is customary to believe that no learning takes place in the church school unless someone is talking. Few teachers feel that they could trust junior highs out of their sight. It is customary to believe that intense discipline and supervision are necessary in the church school. These feelings give much food for thought. They suggest that the entire church school structure and atmosphere may work against the possibility of young people doing their own work. What is needed may be not so much multiplied dictionaries as a change in approach to teaching.

Some of the problems or complaints taken up here—space, time, shared materials—can be met best by changing the meeting time for junior highs to a weekday instead of Sunday morning.

Using audio-visual materials presents some of the same problems taken up under outside resources. For more about this, see the next chapter.

What other questions and/or complaints do you have about the method of teaching outlined in this chapter?

ONE LAST QUESTION

"What about my well-laid plans?" asks a plaintive voice that has been waiting to be heard. "Why did I have to plan so carefully if the junior highs are going to do it all over again?" The simple answer, of course, is that the teacher plans in order to help young adolescents plan. But that is not enough answer for the plaintive voice. He wants to know what will happen if the junior highs come up with ideas he hasn't planned for or if they want to explore questions that hadn't even occurred to him. Many a teacher would panic if they did.

Must the teacher say, "No, we can't do that," and clam up when things take an unexpected direction? He certainly is tempted to do just that. He is always pressed for time, always feeling there is so much to cover. Furthermore, he has a certain justifiable fondness for his own plans, with which he feels somewhat at home. He prefers not to be thrown out into the uncertainty that faces him when new suggestions are made.

But the new may not be so uncertain as it seems at first. If junior highs suggest another way of working, such as the living pictures in the session demonstrated above, they probably know how to do it. For the most part, the young people are more at home with the methods suggested here than teachers are. That is, at least, a measure of comfort.

In the second place, the teacher is not a silent partner in the junior highs' planning. He leads the discussion in which possible ways of working are considered and evaluated. In such work he necessarily sets some standards. Suppose a member of the class suggests a somewhat childish procedure, pasting pictures of Jesus in a scrapbook. Many junior highs, given a chance, would quickly discard the idea because it is childish and seems to have no point. If they do not do so, the teacher raises the questions about why they should make a scrapbook and how it will help in the classwork. The pupil may have been talking off the top of his head and will drop the idea, saying, "I don't know," when faced with such questions. Perhaps, however, he had something more in mind. He meant looking for great art masterpieces because he thought they would be interesting and would contribute something to the class. Then it might be the teacher's turn to suggest that an art exhibit in the classroom—and maybe in the church foyer—would be of more interest and value than pictures pasted in a book. Now the suggestion is in a form that can rightfully be considered by the class. Again, when junior highs suggest a too-ambitious project, it is the teacher who guides the process of evaluating the idea. He raises questions about the amount of work involved and whether or not it is possible.

Thus the teacher has a continually guiding role to play in decisions about classwork. The important decisions are made in terms of what to do, why, how, who will do it, whether it is worth doing. They are not made in terms of "Was this what I (the teacher) had in mind?"

Still other panic-producing problems can arise. Take the case of the pupil who wanted to know about war in the Middle Ages. The teacher redirected the question to one of the relation between war and faith. Perhaps there was in the teacher's background material no article on "War and Faith" or information about the Crusades, one of the more obvious medieval expressions of faith in the form of conflict. Further, there is no session outline that takes up the subject. But here he is, with one pupil assigned the task of finding information, and the question supposedly coming up for discussion at some time or other. Chances are that, if he is fairly well prepared for the unit, the teacher can add this item of exploration or, maybe, substitute it for something in the plans that was not of much interest to the class. It will mean extra reading, extra thinking and planning, but it may well be worth all that.

In any case, the teacher must replan the unit after the planning session with junior highs. He has now found out what they know, what they think, what they can do in a particular subject area. These facts alone will force the teacher to review his plans, to drop some things he had included, to work in things he had not planned, perhaps to take less time over some matters and more time over others.

More often than not, the plans made by the class will look very much like the plans the teacher made. He does know fairly well beforehand what the class will do. This is true because of some simple facts. The subject of study is set; to it the teacher gives a basic direction or focus. Methods are, after all, not limitless, and the teacher soon learns the essentials of most of them. A certain standard of work is in his mind—the very best that the junior highs can do. And he has learned much about the capabilities and the interests of the pupils.

"So," says the cynic, "the junior highs don't really plan. They come out just where you thought they would." And that is entirely possible, because many a teacher can seem to be planning with young people and subtly, all unconsciously, make sure that his plans are not disturbed.

"Oh, well," says the nonbeliever, "it is just a matter of making them feel that they are doing the work." The comment, a very common one, is a useful clue to the fine line that the teacher walks in helping junior highs take responsibility for study—the line between "What do you want to do?" and "Do this! Do that!" For it is not merely a matter of methods. The other side of the matter, and a very important side, has to do with the relationship between teacher and young adolescents. The teacher who only wants to "make them feel" they are responsible—which is to say, wants to put something over on them—may mean that he is not willing to study alongside the pupils.

Reread the section "Planning Ahead for a Unit" in Chapter 6 in the light of the statement, "The teacher plans in order to help junior highs plan."

Consider the comments of the cynic and the nonbeliever. Do their ideas have some validity? Is planning with junior highs merely a trick to make them feel they are doing something?

How would you now define the middle ground between "What do you want to do?" and "Do this! Do that!"? Try explaining to someone else what you mean by helping junior highs plan their own work.

8. Fact-finding

How can the adult help young adolescents develop the background information essential in studying the story of faith?

A BAD REPUTATION

The ways in which junior highs can find out details of time and place are usually known as activities and committees. Activities, unfortunately, suffer from the reputation they have long had in church school work, and "committees" often seems merely a newfangled word for them. One teacher will consider activities as extras, frosting on the cake of the lesson. Another will think they are the reward for getting through the lesson. Still another believes they are opportunities for the teacher, exhausted from his presentation, to relax and let the pupils do something they would like to do for the last few minutes. To many, activities are a way of helping junior highs use up energy that otherwise bothers the teacher. Some identify activities as ways of "making them feel they are doing the work." Almost all teachers say that there is not enough time for them.

But activities in junior high study are always fact-finding work closely related to the subject of study and contributing essential information to the classwork. They are the means by which young people consider the story of faith as history and not as vague generalities.

How do most teachers you know view activities and committees? What idea of teaching underlies the views suggested here? How does it differ from study?

Review quickly the section "Time and Place," in Chapter 4, to remind yourself why details of time and place are essential. Review also the fact-finding activities set up in the demonstration session in Chapter 7.

In order to consider the development and use of such activities, you are invited to guide two parts of a session with junior highs. The session is one in the unit on the Middle Ages, for which plans were made in Chapter 7. This kind of session is more typical of week-to-week work than the planning session.

Assuming that we have reworked our plans for the unit and have carried out the preparation for a session (described in Chapter 6), there is yet one more thing we must do by way of preparation. We must have

An Alarm Clock

The clock may be a real one, timed to get us up early. Or it may be a mental alarm that will get us to class on time. We need an alarm because "on time" for us is fifteen minutes before any junior high arrives. That, of course, may be a half hour before the stated time at which the class is to start.

In the old-style Sunday school class such a practice would have been ridiculous. By reviewing our memories, whether long-standing or as recent as last week, we can see why. The official time for beginning, let us say, is 10:00 o'clock. At 9:50 a few junior highs arrive and sit down to wait in the assembly room. At 9:55 a teacher arrives and more junior highs. At 9:56 the superintendent comes in, busily passes out hymnals, makes preparations for the opening worship. A large group of junior highs arrives next along with a few teachers. The assembly begins at 10:05 while pupils are still arriving. The rest of the teachers and some pupils make it by 10:15.

Perhaps pupils go directly to their classes, which are supposed to start at 10:00, instead of having opening assembly or worship. Those who arrive at 9:50 sit in their classroom and wait for the teacher to come. At 9:55 the teacher arrives and sits with them, waiting for the others to come. With luck, he may feel that there are enough pupils on hand by 10:05 to start the lesson. He may have to start over again at 10:10 and at 10:15, when the rest arrive.

In either case, whether pupils go first to an assembly or first to classes, the essential task for them during about fifteen minutes is waiting around for something to begin. No one can blame young people for being late when they have no more exciting prospect than this facing them. One can hardly blame the teachers; if they come early, most of the pupils are not there. Who can blame the superintendent for wanting to retain the opening assembly because it so neatly covers the general lateness?

Altogether it makes for a great deal of wasted time during which junior highs readily absorb the atmosphere, one of, "Nothing can happen until the teachers (or enough pupils) arrive," with strong overtones of, "Nothing will happen anyhow."

However, we have learned about an entirely different way for church school to begin, which makes it necessary for us to have an alarm clock. We do not have an assembly or large-group worship in our church school hour. Neither do we have a lesson to begin when there are enough pupils present. In other words, we have no cover for tardiness. We get there early.

During the few minutes that we are alone we find plenty to do. We check the resource-books center, maybe adding slips of paper at specific references the pupils are to use. Perhaps, if we have to remove the books each week, we must lay them out. We check over supplies and put out directions for the work groups.

We have these household duties barely under way when

The First Pupil Arrives

Ernest Early, we can guess, is the only one in his home who gets up on Sunday morning, and he becomes bored around the house. Ernest is one of the committee that is finding out about the everyday life of people in medieval times. We remind him of the fact, refer him to the work outline, point out to him the sources of information, maybe suggest a particular one or give him an even more specific direction of something to look for. We may not need to give him so much guidance; he may be ready to go to work on his own. Ernest starts his work, accompanied by suitable conversation between him and us about anything or about the work at hand.

Two girls arrive just as we have Ernest started on his work, and we help them start also. By the time the other pupils come the room is humming, and we have difficulty in not spinning like a top.

Work on the fact-finding activities might proceed for a short or a long time according to what needs to be done and what we have planned for other parts of the session. No one has noticed when the class began and, indeed, whether it has begun. But *work* began, as it should, as soon as there were a pupil and a teacher.

While the junior highs are at work we are not idle. We are engaged in

Supervision of Several Activities

Our first responsibility is to help everyone get started, as we did with Ernest.

When Susie, who is self-motivating, arrives, she shows us a picture that she drew and goes to work without prompting.

Eloise, however, sits down at the table and looks vague, partly because she has forgotten from one week to the next what she was to do. Also, the two others on her committee have not yet come and she is not one to start without them. We sit down to work with Eloise a few minutes. Perhaps we begin by asking her what her work group was doing last week, because she probably can remember. Then, instead of ordering her to work, we take an oblique approach. It does not just happen that we know Eloise was looking for a picture of a castle room but could not find what she wanted. Neither does it just happen that we came across a good picture and brought it to add to the resources. We are ready to direct Eloise to a source of information. We do not put it into her hands as though she were a child, but we expect her to find it on her own once we have told her it is available on the resource table. We shall check later as to how she uses it. By that time the others in the work group will have arrived so that Eloise can have some support.

Here is Ed, who was absent last week. Probably the best thing will be to let him join his work group and see whether he can pick up where he left off two weeks ago. Or maybe we should work with the group a few minutes to review what they are doing so that Ed can fit back into the work.

Paul, who is a conscientious worker and a "loner," is looking up facts on medieval architecture. Our few minutes of work with him are directed to helping him limit himself in what is a big field. This is the time to plan with him a way to prepare his report to the class. We suggest he find pictures and make a poster that he can explain to the others. Admittedly we are suggesting a rather simple procedure, but without something that specific Paul is likely to read to the class an entire encyclopedia article which he found fascinating.

Back to Ernest's everyday-life committee for more than a few minutes, because the committee is to present its information today. Last week we helped the group plan a way to report. They are going to project a short filmstrip for which they have written a script based on information they looked up. A run-through of the presentation is going on. It has just occurred to members of the committee that they need an extra person to run the projector. They have borrowed Tom from another committee. Tom seems pleased to help, and the committee he was borrowed from is proceeding smoothly. We are not especially anxious, therefore, to send him back where he belongs but accept the new arrangement. We listen to the rehearsal, commenting only on the quality of the presentation, whether it is understandable, can be heard, and the like. It is too late now to ask for any revision in the script even though we have an uneasy feeling that important information has been omitted. Because of our uneasiness, we ask, "Will members of the committee let other pupils ask questions after the presentation?" Well—oh, sure—but suppose they ask something we don't know—we'll tell them where to look it up.

It begins to become clear, doesn't it, why the teacher must resist the temptation to spin like a top? At least it is clear that the teacher in this kind of work is on his feet and circulating. He will be if the class is large and has a room or space of its own. If space is limited to one table with chairs around it, the teacher may still circulate by looking over shoulders, or he may sit in the middle of the long side of the table and work across it with the committees in turn. Or he moves unobtrusively along the length of the pew, sitting with each work group for a while. In any case, it is the teacher's responsibility to spend some time with each working group or individual.

His further responsibilities are to:

—*know beforehand what each work group planned to do and has done so far.* It is only such detailed knowledge in the teacher's notes or in his head that can prevent topspinning.

—*get work under way,* often by asking the members of the group to tell what they have done and what they are ready to do now.

—*help plan a way of working and keep the committee to it.* In many cases, it is well to have a written outline or plan of work. Sometimes these are available in the curriculum materials. Sometimes they are made out by the work groups themselves or written by the teacher on the basis of ideas brought out in the planning session. With a work plan at hand, both the teacher and the junior highs have a way to check progress and to work toward a goal. In addition, the work then belongs to the group and is being done not for the teacher but to fulfill the purposes agreed on by members of the committee.

—*challenge the junior highs to make use of their skills.* Fact-finding is not like painting a picture by filling in numbered spaces with the right colors. It is more like painting a picture of your own. There is much room for creativity. Specific suggestions, whether in print or drawn up from the teacher's ideas or from those of the pupils, are only suggestions and stimuli to the abilities of young people. The teacher is the one who helps each young person find what he can do and work up to his capacity, whether the capacity is small or great.

—and, at the same time, *keep the work within limits.* The limits are generally set by the use to be made of the information. It is well to urge a work group to move rather quickly toward planning a way to present its findings to the rest of the class. Having to decide what will be presented and how helps to keep a group from carelessly deciding to build a complete scale-model cathedral, for example (a project that would take the rest of the year and might or might not contribute to classwork).

—*know and constantly point junior highs to the resources* in which they can find information. Sometimes, when they use large books or adult books, it is necessary for the teacher to make out reference slips showing pages and paragraphs that are to be used. For the most part, however, junior highs know how to use tables of contents, indexes, encyclopedias, and libraries, as well as how to skim a text until they come to the information needed. Teachers do not need to be spoon-feeders.

—*have in mind a store of methods,* especially for the presentation of information, and make them available to the work groups. Such a store may be built up out of ideas gained from advance preparation of the unit and out of the teacher's gatherings from previous units.

—*put to work in other ways pupils whose committee work has come to an end.* For example, after Ernest Early's committee reports, there will be three young people to plan for. The teacher may suggest another way of using the information the committee has gathered. In this case they presented a filmstrip with a script of their own. Maybe they would also like to make large drawings to put around the classroom. Perhaps they should be put to work preparing for a session yet to come. They might prepare a play-reading about Francis of Assisi from a dramatization supplied for the session two weeks later.

—*keep track of time,* and in the light of where groups are in their work, call a halt. Usually the teacher has in mind an approximate amount of time for committee or small-group work and when he will bring it to an end. Just as usually, he must make the decision on the spot, regardless of what he had planned to do. The stopping time has to be gauged to allow enough time for satisfactory work, but, except for a committee reporting in that session, work does not have to come to completion. It will be taken up again the next week. Because some work groups may not be able to bring their activities to an immediate halt, it is well to give a three- to five-minute warning. Time must be allowed for gathering up materials, returning books to the resource table or library, putting away supplies, and the like. All these activities are the responsibility of the junior highs. The teacher may help, but he should not get into the habit of doing it all for them.

A Change of Pace

Leaving the everyday-life committee, we now make a tour of all the groups to see where they are in their work. Most of them are at or near good stopping points. We tell each one that it has about three minutes more to finish work and put things away.

We call all the members of the class together and ask them to bring chairs and make a circle beside the worktable. (If we do not have enough space for a circle, we gather around the table. In the case of a class limited to sitting around a table or limited to a pew, the "gathering" of the class would mean getting unneeded materials out of the way and focusing attention.)

Then we proceed to a

Report from a Committee

In our work today the junior highs are to take the parts of different medieval people, parts that they may take throughout the unit—a possibility that is not yet definite because we are waiting to see how the young people take to the idea. Descriptions of several medieval people are given in the pupils' notebook. We assign them to different pupils. We ask the young people to get acquainted with "themselves" and to be ready to tell about themselves as medieval people later in the session. We also say that, after they have read the descriptions, the committee on everyday life will help us imagine in more detail what it was like to live then.

A few minutes of silent, individual work follow. Ernest Early and his fellow committee members are giving a last-minute look at their script. Tom is checking the projector and screen to make sure they have not been moved out of line. We interrupt the reading pupils to present the committee on everyday life. The members of the committee, plus Tom, show the short filmstrip and give some information related to each frame. They tell about dress, homes, furniture, people such as knights and clergy, education, occupations.

After their presentation, we review briefly the important points they brought out. Then we ask the other members of the class whether they have questions to put to the committee. One pupil points out that the majority of people were not of the nobility or the clergy but were serfs. It dawns on the three members of the committee that they have left something important out of their report. But they had looked up information about serfs, so Ernest says, "I'm glad you asked that question," and tells what he knows about serfs.

Another member of the class wants to know what vows knights took. The members of the committee do not know; neither do we. But one committee member thinks he knows where he can find out and volunteers to do so. We make a note of this, because if we don't, we are likely to forget and leave him prepared to make a contribution that we never ask him for.

The pupil who wanted to know about war (when we were planning the unit) says he wishes the committee had said more about war. The members of the committee point out to him that he himself is looking up that subject. The persistent pupil, pleased to have the matter thrown back at him, is ready to say something about war. However, we feel that he is not really ready to report and that his information will be more useful in a later session. We suggest that he wait.

When discussion of the report slacks off we suggest that the pupils take a few more minutes to prepare their introductions of themselves as medieval people. Now, we point out, they can use not only the information in the descriptions but also what they have learned from the committee presentation.

In its work periods the committee on everyday life found information, put it together, prepared a report, and rehearsed its report. In presenting the report, these pupils supplied for others in the class information they needed in order to identify themselves with members of the church in the past.

What are the teacher's responsibilities in the presentation and use of reports from fact-finding groups? He is responsible for:

—*variety in methods of reporting.* The word "report" immediately and most frequently calls to mind the picture of a junior high standing before the class telling the others what he found out. Simple oral reports are frequently used but they become monotonous if overused. The teacher is responsible for helping pupils find different ways to report.

The committee on everyday life combined projected material with an oral report. Another work group might mount pictures on a poster. Members of the committee might take time to explain the poster or might merely hang it in the classroom for others to refer to. Still another group might make a series of small posters each with a picture (drawn or mounted) and a paragraph of information. These could be added to the resource materials for the pupils to use. Another committee might put its information in the form of a word-list chart (or, in the case of work on Bible material, a continuing Bible dictionary). A group might plan a special service of worship, using forms and materials from medieval times, and lead the others in the service. Others might teach a hymn. A group might make a collection of prayers and mimeograph copies for members of the class. In order to share its information a committee might plan and present an interview between a modern young person and a young person of medieval times. A brief dramatization may be the best way for another fact-finding group to report.

There are many possible ways to report. They are the sort of methods the teacher must begin to store in his memory as he supervises fact-finding work.

—introduction of the report and integration with class-work. It is the teacher who sets the stage, that is, demonstrates the need for the report and works it into the class procedure. There is no point in having pupils listen to a report if the information given is not needed at that time. What was needed in this session was more detail about life in medieval times so that junior highs would be able to imagine themselves as people living then. The report was introduced by having the pupils begin to get acquainted with some information. In hearing the report, they were given an opportunity to gain more information and were directed to make use of it in follow-up work.

A report on war, which the persistent pupil was eager to give, while of relevance to the everyday life of medieval people, would really be of more use to the class at another time. Thus it is put off, even though the teacher may be tempted to give way to the eagerness of the persistent pupil.

—*the use of information given in a report.* While a report is being given, the teacher follows it carefully, noting what is presented. Almost always he helps by reviewing, emphasizing, or restating information given in the report. He does this either in a brief statement of his own or in questions directed to the class, usually by a combination of both. For example, the teacher might start by saying, "The committee told us about three classes of people in medieval times: nobles, clergy, and serfs. What did it tell us about the nobles?" Or, "If you had lived then, which class would you have wanted to belong to?" To give more depth to information presented, the teacher might note, in speaking of different kinds of people, that classes were much more rigid in those days than they are today.

The listening ear of the teacher must also catch what the reporters omit. In the case of the everyday-life committee's report, it was clear beforehand that there was an omission of important information. It was too late to make a correction without upsetting the entire report. The teacher, in such a case, would be prepared to ask the committee to expand its report by telling about the missing item, information the junior highs probably have but overlooked in planning the report. Often other pupils will question and correct the information in a report, as happened in this session. At times, the teacher himself would supply the missing information.

The teacher is listening also in terms of how the information given can be used by the class. Facts presented by the everyday-life committee were directed to an immediate use in helping the pupils imagine what kind of people they would have been in medieval times. In this case, things proceeded fairly smoothly. The matter is not always so simple.

—*recapture of inadequate reports*. Reports can go astray for various reasons. It may not be immediately apparent to the other pupils how they are to use the information given. Suppose Paul, preparing a report on medieval architecture to be used when the class "visits" a cathedral, cannot be led away from his technical interest. He presents a detailed report on the engineering feats accomplished in building the cathedrals. It is interesting information and Paul has done good work, both of which facts the teacher mentions first. Meantime, the other pupils are baffled because none of them share Paul's technical interests and abilities. The teacher is inwardly thinking, Where do we go from here?

A possible way would be to question both Paul and the other pupils on how and by whom these feats were performed, thus leading back to the medieval people who, in many cases, built the cathedrals. Maybe at this point the teacher can ask Paul or someone to find quickly and pass around pictures that show what the engineering feats looked like to those who worshiped in them.

The teacher will be faced with the greatest need for improvisation, as well as tact, in making use of reports carelessly prepared or presented. He may need to move quickly in order to protect the reporting committee or pupil from the scorn of other pupils who recognize the inadequacy of the work. They will sometimes bluntly point it out. The teacher, of course, is already casting about for ways to fill in the gap. It would be a mistake at such a moment to call on a star pupil to give the right answers or to hand things over completely to those in the class who would mercilessly show up the committee.

Perhaps no teacher can or should fully protect pupils against correction from fellow pupils for careless and inadequate work. But it would be better for the teacher to give the needed information himself. He can start by acknowledging anything of value, however slight, in the report. On that basis he can build additional information—"It is also true that . . ." or, "Another fact about . . ."

Difficulties can arise because of unequal abilities. For example, a pupil who is unaccustomed to this kind of work or has limited reading ability makes a report by showing some pictures he has found. Other pupils think the report is simpleminded. Then the teacher must stand between the pupil who worked up to his capacity and others who have more ability. He must make the report valid no matter how simple it was by showing the class how to make use of the information instead of bypassing it. He might, for example, insist that the pictures be passed around so that everyone gets a closer look at them. While the pictures circulate, he reviews what the pupil said (or perhaps did not say, letting the pictures speak for him) by suggesting things to look for in the pictures. The reporting pupil will not be surprised; that is just what he meant to say but couldn't. Others who were critical may be surprised to find there was more to the report than they thought.

However, in all cases of inadequate or carelessly done reports, the teacher should look to himself also. Perhaps better supervision of the work by him would have prevented the situation. He might have caught the omission of information at an earlier time when it could still be corrected. The suggestion made to Paul about using pictures may have been a mistake. Perhaps he rejected it because it was too simple for him. Lacking any other ideas, he fell back on what he would feel most satisfied in doing.

Looking back on the parts of a session "we" have guided and the analysis of them, how would you describe the role of the teacher?

Go back over the material and mark or list methods that are new to you ($\checkmark$), suggestions that seem strange to you (?), and things you feel you could not possibly do (X). In regard to the last list, ask yourself why you couldn't. If it is a matter of space, time, or materials, reread the section "Some Questions and/or Complaints" in Chapter 7. If it is a matter of never having tried the suggested methods, the best remedy is trying them.

To get the feel of the kind of work suggested here, you might plan a teachers meeting at which everyone is assigned to a work group, carries out fact-finding work (as suggested in curriculum materials), including a report, as though they were junior highs. It is not necessary to act like junior highs, since adults cannot, no matter how hard they try.

CONTRASTS

Many teachers are baffled when they first see, hear of, or read about the ways of working suggested here. They are baffled not so much by difficult, new methods as by a conflict. It is the conflict between their ideas of teaching and the views of teaching that underlie the new methods.

Mrs. One-Book has always thought teaching centered in a textbook, the contents of which are to be mastered by the pupils.

Mr. Lecture sees teaching as an address, combining information and inspiration, made by himself to assembled pupils.

Miss Recitation thinks of a question-answer routine in which the pupils give back to her what they have learned. She searches for the right answers and rewards those who can give them.

Mr. Drill regards teaching as repetition. The facts are presented to the pupils, reviewed, recited, memorized until known.

Miss Competition sees the class as a place where pupils strive to outdo one another in their mastery of knowledge, thus keeping each other up to the mark.

Mrs. Free-Discussion believes in talking everything over. The pupils express their ideas on a subject until they come to some kind of agreement.

In contrast, the teacher who adopts the ways of working suggested here:

—makes available to the pupils several sources of information, an approach with which junior highs are usually more familiar than are their church school teachers.

—understands that junior highs learn in other ways than listening.

—wants young people to be exposed to as many facts as possible, rather than to a few that are to be memorized.

—is concerned that pupils should find accurate information for reasons of integrity rather than for the hope of a reward on producing the right answers.

—sees that junior highs are to use facts as a step along the way, not as goals to be reached.

—helps the pupils use information as the background for identification and for thinking, considering, weighing, rather than material to be mastered by drill.

—plans for give-and-take from pupil to pupil and does not rely solely on teacher to pupil and pupil to teacher give-and-take.

—is willing to allow young people to make their own mistakes and learn from them, free of the pressure of "being right."

—gives everyone an opportunity for satisfaction in his own work, rather than rewarding only those who are gifted with good memories.

—stresses what each junior high can contribute to the class, instead of "star" performances.

—holds pupils to a standard of the best work each can do rather than to an absolute standard of achievement.

—knows that, in order to discuss, junior highs must first be informed by a background of facts; otherwise they are only talking over their ignorance.

How you were taught is the most determinative factor in how you will teach. You may find it helpful to recall in as much detail as possible how you were taught. Was it in one of the ways suggested here?

Contrast each of the ways of teaching illustrated by Mrs. One-Book and the others with the methods of study, according to: the relationship between pupils and teachers, the relationships among pupils, the use of factual information, the physical arrangement of a class (drawings or diagrams will show the difference).

Many teachers cling to methods which restrict give-and-take to that between teacher and pupil. What do you think are the reasons: familiarity with such methods? desire for authority? a wish to avoid uncertainty? fear of adolescents? a Sunday school tradition of the need for strict discipline? a certain view of faith? inability to abandon the role of a parent? other?

You have considered in detail two steps in study, planning, and fact-finding. Before reading further, you may want to reread Chapter 4, beginning with the section "The Basic Method: Living Into," in order to recall the reasons that underlie specific methods.

Audio-Visuals: Ooh! and Ugh!

Ernest and his fellow committee members presented their report as a script they had written for a short filmstrip. "Uh-huh," reacts many a teacher, knowing full well that no such thing would be possible in his class.

The way it usually goes with audio-visuals is: The whole department meets or the juniors and junior highs meet together in order to make it worthwhile to have a film or filmstrip. Class work is curtailed or omitted, usually with no advance notice given to teachers. There is a lot of squirming around while everyone waits for the show to begin. The center of the room is taken up by a projector with wires going off in all directions. Everyone forgets that fact, so there is much tripping and stumbling. An outsider is on hand to run the projector. At the last minute he finds he must adjust the screen, unwind more cords, focus the projector, turn it off again. Someone turns the room lights off and on again. A teacher moves to pull down the shades. Four pupils jump up to help, there being only two windows. Finally, amid mounting restlessness the lights go off, the projector is on, and the audio-visual is under way. When it is over, everyone gets up blinking and goes out dazed enough to trip over the cords lying about.

These are, more or less, the impressions that come to mind when audio-visual materials are mentioned. It is no wonder that everyone considers them marvels of modern Christian education, while almost no one uses them. The difficulty is that audio-visuals are considered to be (and in practice are) something brought in from the outside, extras requiring special arrangements, outside experts, general disruption. Almost no one looks at audio-visual aids from within the teaching situation itself.

Mrs. Dalton is an innocent when she begins teaching. That is to say, she has had almost nothing to do with church schools before. Therefore, she has never had any disheartening experiences with audio-visuals, and no one has told her of the difficulties she might face.

When she is listing and assembling materials for a unit, she finds among the things mentioned a filmstrip of which twenty frames relate to the work the junior highs will be doing. She borrows the strip and a projector from the church. To the considerable enjoyment of her husband and children, she projects the twenty frames on the living room wall one evening. It is clear to Mrs. Dalton that the junior highs would get some valuable information from seeing these frames. She decides to use them in the planning session in order to give the pupils a preview of the unit.

It might fit, she thinks, after the looking-around time and some exploratory discussion. The things they talk over could well lead into looking at the filmstrip, she reasons. Then they might discuss it afterward. A good first question might be, "What interested you most?" Or, how about, "Would you like to have lived then?"

Mrs. Dalton makes arrangements to use the filmstrip and a projector. The person in charge of equipment lays out a screen also, but Mrs. Dalton decides not to use it. No room, she thinks. It would be better to use the wall. The audio-visual person also offers to come and run the projector. "Oh, no, thank you," says Mrs. Dalton, the innocent. "I can do it myself."

She goes to church early, gets out the projector, places it at one side of the class table, threads the filmstrip, focuses it, and runs it through to the first frame of the series she wants to show. Then she pictures in her mind whether all the pupils can see the image if their chairs are rearranged. Now that everything is ready, she turns off the machine.

At the right moment in the session, Mrs. Dalton suggests that the young people look at a few frames of a filmstrip. She tells briefly what the frames show, suggests things the junior highs should look for, the things they found they did not know in the preceding discussion. While Mrs. Dalton turns on the projector, a pupil pulls down the window shade. She reads the script as she clicks the frames in place. After the projector is turned off, the teacher and pupils talk over what they saw, new things they learned, how they could learn more.

At the end of class time Mrs. Dalton is talking at the doorway with one of the girls. When she turns back she finds Ted playing, it seems, with the projector. But it turns out that Ted is not playing; he knows very well what he is doing. "Mrs. Dalton, you know that picture of a shepherd? I just wanted to see it again." He has already found the right frame. He seems to know how to handle both the machine and the film with care. That, he explains, is because he is on a projection committee in school and does this sort of thing often. Ted helps Mrs. Dalton put the projector in its case. He discovers a small screen that can be clipped to the opposite end of the projector case and shows his teacher how it is used.

Mrs. Dalton begins to put these facts together. Ted wanted to see one picture over again. He can competently handle the mechanics of doing so. There is a small screen that could be used for tabletop viewing.

When the junior highs come to class the next week, they find among the resource materials the projector with a filmstrip in it threaded to the first of the series of pictures they had seen the week before and focused on the small screen. Mrs. Dalton points out these new tools, suggesting that different committees might like to take a second look at the sequence of frames or at one picture. She is ready to make even more specific suggestions of frames the committees might find helpful. Ted has been asked to stand by and help because Mrs. Dalton is not sure all the junior highs know how to take care of the film. She also asks Ted to show the others how to do so, as well as a few other essentials of good projection.

This innocent teacher, having no background of discouraging experiences, is not "using audio-visuals." She is merely meeting a need for information by using every resource available to her.

One of the best uses of audio-visual materials—viewed from within the teaching situation—is for making information available. Filmstrips are usually better adapted to such use than films. Generally speaking, filmstrips are planned for teaching purposes. Some documentary and informational films are also, but, for the most part, church-produced films tend to be storytelling and inspirational. They have their uses—for example, in discussion of issues —but fact-finding in study with junior highs is not one of them.

In order to use audio-visuals within the teaching situation, the teacher *must:*

—*search for items that give information.* Part of a filmstrip may be the item. For example, in a filmstrip that surveys the Old Testament, there may be ten frames about Moses. There is no point in showing all fifty-six frames of the strip if it is information about Moses that is needed. They make a good "show," but three fifths of them are irrelevant at that time.

—*become familiar with the material beforehand* so that he can know exactly what is in it and how it can be used.

—*practice the technique of using a filmstrip,* correlating script and frames, making the smoothest possible arrangements for turning off lights, turning on the projector, and the like. All such details should be taken care of beforehand, so that members of the class do not sit around doing nothing while things are set up and tried out. If these details must be done during class time, they should be carried out while junior highs are busy at something else, not after they have gathered together to look at the film.

—*work out a way to introduce the audio-visual material,* including hints on how it will help, a brief statement of what it shows, and usually something that the pupils should be looking for, such as facts, answers to a question, or things not known before.

—*decide on a good first question to use after the showing.* Often it can be, "What did you find most interesting?" A few tentative follow-through questions should be planned also, but once started, the discussion of what was seen usually proceeds on its own.

When the teacher uses audio-visuals within the teaching situation, it is possible:

—*for him to run the projector himself* without having an outside expert.

—*for junior highs to learn how to handle projection;* some of them already know.

—*to project on surfaces other than a large screen,* which should be used only with a large class. Small-scale projection is better if the class is small. Some projectors are equipped with small screens. If the wall is to be used, as it often can be, projection should be checked in daylight conditions to make sure it is possible. In some cases, an opaque screen is better. The image is projected through an opaque screen, and viewers sit facing the projector, rather than between it and the screen. It is also possible to make or to have made a small screen to clip on the end of a table.

—*to reuse all or parts of the material.* This is one of the great advantages of the filmstrip. Provided the projector has a fan so that the film will not be burned, it is possible to stop and linger over one frame for further information or discussion. Probably on the first showing, the teacher does better to follow the script provided or to use the recorded sound, if any. After that, he can turn back to specific frames for further exploration.

Also, when sections of a filmstrip are used with particular units, it is possible at a later time to show the entire strip for reviewing or fitting things into a larger picture. Junior highs do not usually object to the reuse of material, provided that it has been used from the beginning for teaching purposes and not as a "show."

—*to rewrite the script.* Sometimes the teacher will want to do so instead of using the script or sound provided. He should prepare a written script and not rely on his ability to talk at random about each frame.

—*for junior highs to write a script of their own.* The script that Ernest's committee wrote accompanied a strip that had only brief captions on each frame and no script. What the young people did was to expand each caption. They could follow a similar procedure if the strip had an accompanying script, expanding it and emphasizing additional information.

—*to make a filmstrip available for junior highs to use* either entirely or in part *in their fact-finding work.* If the pictures give authentic details, say, of New Testament times, the junior highs may want to refer to them for many purposes.

Both class use and pupil use of audio-visual materials, as suggested here, assume that more equipment is available than most churches have. It sounds as though every class has its own projector—which may soon be possible as less expensive machines come on the market. In reality, there is usually one projector and one copy of a filmstrip available for the use of many classes. Careful scheduling is essential if teachers are to make teaching uses of audiovisuals. If a certain filmstrip is suggested for a unit, per-

haps only one class can use it in the opening session. Another class will have to use it in the second session. A
third may schedule it for use in the final session of the unit
as review.

It is possible for two or even three classes to use the
same material on one day, not by getting together for the
viewing, but by careful preplanning and by having someone unobtrusively move the equipment from one room
to another. For example, pupils in one class might use a
filmstrip for fact-finding work at the beginning of the hour.
When they come to the end of the work the filmstrip and
equipment would be transferred to another class for use
at a later point in the session.

Most teachers who get interested in teaching uses of
audio-visuals find that the way is clear for them. Investi-
gation usually shows that audio-visuals, if available in the
church at all, are very much available, because no one is
making use of them.

Is it never possible to use audio-visuals with several
classes together? Yes, it is possible, provided:

—all arrangements are made beforehand so that it is
never necessary for a large group of young people to suffer
through last-minute setting-up exercises.

—the material to be used is related to current teaching.
Too often what happens is that the church rents a film for
the senior highs to use at an evening meeting. Someone
feels it is necessary to get their money's worth out of the
film, so why not show it to the junior highs too. (Or the
telephone company makes available free films and it's too
good an opportunity to miss.) The entire work of the department comes to a halt while a show is put on. Few
adults realize how boring this use of audio-visuals can be
to young people. Films and the like are no novelty to them.
That is why they are better used for teaching purposes
than for miscellaneous showing which someone thinks
will be a treat for the junior highs.

—all the teachers plan together beforehand so that a
suitable introduction is made either in classes or in the

large group—one that fits with teaching purposes and
needs—and each one can lead a follow-through discussion *in his own class.*

What impressions does the term "audio-visuals" bring to
your mind?
Look through your teaching materials for suggested audio-
visual materials. Resolutely putting out of mind all your previous experiences with audio-visuals, plan how you might use
a suggested resource: in the first planning session of a unit, for
junior highs to use in fact-finding, as review in the last session.
To do so you will need to start with the plan for the session
and see how the audio-visual material can be used within it.
If you are working with other teachers, plan to spend a meeting on one projected item available in your church, preferably
one related to the current subject of study. After they have
looked at it, let everyone "brainstorm"—that is, suggest things
off the tops of their heads—about possible ways to use it.
Make a list of the brainstorming results, then consider in more
detail the uses, introduction, follow-through discussion. Ask
someone to demonstrate small-scale projection, if possible. This
would be a good time, also, to give every teacher a chance to
learn the techniques of projection.

9. Learning to Read

How can the adult help young adolescents learn to read the Bible with understanding?

A SIMPLE ANSWER

Junior highs learn to read the Bible by reading it, which, in turn, means that adults should help them make actual use of the Bible in classwork. What an obvious basic principle—one that is not widely carried out in practice.

Suppose an interviewer asked six dozen teachers about the importance of the Bible in the church school. They would all agree that it is very important. Not a few would express their conviction that "more Bible" is needed. If the researcher inquired further as to how the Bible should be taught, he would find himself with six dozen different answers. Of the answers, no more than three would be related to helping young people learn to read.

In the first place, having junior highs read in the Bible takes time, more time than the teacher thinks can be given to it. Therefore, he looks for short cuts. Sometimes he gives the gist of a Bible passage without expecting the pupils to read it. If he does allow young people to read for themselves, he too often assumes that the meaning of a passage can become clear in some magical way, without any work needed for understanding.

In the second place, the traditional methods that the teacher has at hand are directed toward "knowing the Bible" or "applying the Bible to life." Thus, confronted with a long passage for study, the teacher tends to want to extract from it a key verse for memorizing. Or he will plan to have the junior highs discuss the lesson of the passage and how they can carry it out in life. These two methods, and many more like them, are directed toward finding in the Bible immediately comprehensible and useful knowledge. They are in no way related to the lifelong involvement of the Christian with Scripture. Indeed, they cut the ground from under any such possibility. The usual aims and practices of the church school are so divergent from the possibility of study that "junior highs reading the Bible" will mean, to most teachers, the individual young person's devotional reading at home.

The teacher who sets out to help young adolescents read the Bible with understanding will have to learn and use entirely different methods.

Review Chapter 3 to recall why study is not directed toward immediately comprehensible and useful knowledge extracted from the Bible.

For a rundown of some approaches and methods commonly used, see the section "Is Study This?" in Chapter 4. How would you describe the aim in each of these methods of "teaching the Bible"? In what ways do they cut the ground from under the possibility of lifelong involvement with the Scriptures?

CERTAIN BASICS

The Bible, being a book, has many similarities to other books. The content of the Bible is unlike that of other books; the relationship of believers to this book is a singular one. But these facts do not change the Bible into something magical. Reading it requires some of the same skills used in approaching any written material, as well as a few special skills. It also requires the use of the understanding.

Right away anyone can see that it is nearly impossible to approach the Bible as a book like any other. The teacher has only to look at the Bibles that junior highs use in class and put them alongside textbooks they use in school. He can see immediately that asking the young person to read in the Bible presents some difficulties. Printers of Bibles have a severe problem, namely, how to get all the text into some handy-sized, usable form. The usual means of meeting the problem are small type and thin paper. Often, when teachers complain that their pupils cannot read, they are overlooking the fact that junior highs have to struggle with unfamiliar small type and a general blurring. Even adults find these are handicaps in reading the Bible. The very format of many editions of the Bible tends to keep it a closed book.

A few editions of the Bible are available in larger type and on better paper. Usually they are too expensive for a church to provide them either as gifts to the young people or for class use. The teacher who doesn't want to take these problems lying down could inquire about a class supply of readable Bibles. Tradition supposes it is nice for the young person to bring "his own" Bible to class, but this is mere sentimentality. If supplying Bibles in class means more readability, then sentiment ought not to stand in the way. There are available also portions of the Bible in better print, some in notebook form. These are often useful because they can be marked and underlined in ways that most young people would not do with their own copies or with class copies.

However, most teachers will not be able to supply anything but the small-type, thin-paper editions. Therefore, the teacher must be aware of the difficulties junior highs encounter when they read in the Bible and never assume that it is easy to do. He had better censor his feelings that the schools are not teaching children to read nowadays. The only truth in that opinion may be that schools are not teaching children to read fine print. Unfortunately, church schools are stuck with having to do so. It requires time and patience, and perhaps acknowledging with junior highs the inevitable difficulties.

Books are commonly divided in various ways into volumes, chapters, sections, and the like. The Bible is, of course, more than a book; it is a collection of books. No teacher of junior highs should expect pupils to have a very broad or knowledgeable acquaintance with the divisions of this collection of books. They have not yet made enough use of it to have gained such familiarity. Most junior highs have been making use of the Bible once a week or so for a matter of four or five years, at the most, six. It is foolish to expect them to find their way around the many books of the Bible from memory.

What happens when the teacher discovers that young adolescents are rather slow and fumbling at finding references in the Bible? If he is wedded to tradition, he deplores the fact that they don't teach anything in the junior department anymore, and devotes several class sessions to drilling the junior highs in the books of the Bible. However, this wastes a great deal of time, because the work of memorizing bears no relation to the work of finding references, and, by its nature, never can. Every copy of the Bible has a table of contents. There is no reason young people should not be trained to use it, just as they would use the table of contents in any large book with numerous parts. The aim of knowing the books of the Bible, rather than a beginning point, should be a late product of many years of familiarity with the Bible. The way to help young adolescents find references is in finding references.

There are other needed skills that the teacher should approach with equal straightforwardness, keeping in mind that the Bible is a book. One of these concerns the matter of abbreviations for the books used in most references to Bible passages. Usually they are the same as the abbreviations for books given in the table of contents of the Bibles used in class (there may be a few variations). Again, the teacher should refer pupils to the table of contents to find for themselves the meanings of abbreviations. However, he should be alert to confusions, and help junior highs connect abbreviations with the full titles of books. Another matter is the way references are written. The usual reference reads, for example, *I Chron. 6:1–7*. This shorthand consists of: the name of the book (usually abbreviated), the chapter number, followed by verse numbers (the hyphen means from verse 1 to the end of verse 7). Most junior highs have some familiarity with the standard form used for references. A few may need help, and many will need help with variations of it. The common variations are *I Chron., ch. 6* (meaning the entire chapter), *I Chron. 6:1 ff.* (meaning verse 1 and a few verses following), *I Chron. 6:13 to 7:5* (meaning to read from a point in one chapter on into another chapter), *I Chron. 6:12b–17* ("b" refers to the second half of verse 12, usually a sentence in itself, which is the beginning point rather than the first, or "a," part of the verse). Often, when the name of a book has already been given, additional references are made without repeating it. These will appear as ch., v., or vs., all rather mysterious to young people when they first see them.

It helps to remember that verse numbers in the Bible were assigned arbitrarily a few centuries ago. They are only a helpful device and have no significance in themselves. Often a numbered verse includes more than one sentence. Sometimes, in terms of meaning, the beginning of a new paragraph occurs in the middle of a verse. A similar thing is true of chapter divisions within books. They are divisions arbitrarily made for easier use. Often the beginning of a new chapter does not coincide with what would be the opening of a new chapter in terms of meaning or content.

One of the chief reasons for having young people use modern versions of the Bible lies in a better handling of the matter of chapters and verses. Older versions are usually printed verse by verse, giving the impression that each verse is a paragraph, important in itself. Modern versions are more often printed in paragraph form according to meaning, with less emphasis on separate verses. The numbers are retained, but usually minimized.

A common error made by junior highs in reading the Bible is finding the right verse in the wrong chapter. The headings at the tops of the pages mislead them. Many young people, on making such a mistake, read stolidly on even though what they read makes little sense (evidence that they have been conditioned to think the Bible is not understandable in any event). Until the teacher is sure of the skills of junior highs, he should probably check frequently and individually whenever the pupils are to find and read a Bible passage. Because there are times when different pupils work with different passages, there is no point in making a class-wide checkup. While the junior highs are finding the passages on their own, the teacher can unobtrusively look over shoulders. It is not necessary to ask each pupil whether he has found the place. As junior highs become accustomed to the teacher's availability and to reading for understanding, they will know where to turn for help when they find themselves reading something that makes no sense.

In no case are any of these skills, such as reading references or finding books, material for drill. Brief explanations may be needed occasionally. Otherwise it should not be necessary to spend any class time on the skills, as such. Junior highs should be mastering them within the process of studying Bible material. Nor should any of the fundamental skills be fodder for competition. The old game of raising hands as each finds the passage is out of place, as are all other similar contests. They are time-consuming practices that do not contribute to study.

Reading in the Bible should be done silently by individual pupils, with very few exceptions. There are a number of reasons for avoiding the practice of reading aloud. Few junior highs are sufficiently skilled to read the Bible aloud in a way that makes it comprehensible to hearers. Even having the teacher read aloud is not efficient. Everyone knows that it is easy to listen while the mind is occupied with some other matter. Young people give closer attention and gain better comprehension from silent reading. They absorb new and strange words more easily in a visual context than in hearing. Silent study allows each pupil to go at his own pace, to reread if necessary, to stop and think. Usually the pupil, either alone or with others, is asked to do something beyond the mere reading, such as to answer a question or to think about an issue. Thus it is not necessary to have an idle waiting period while everyone finishes reading before work can go on. The teacher learns to estimate the amount of time needed for reading and for subsequent individual or group work, and allows that much time.

The practice of reading aloud verse by verse around the class should be avoided. Individual Bible verses are parts of a sequence of meaning; they often have no meaning in themselves. Reading them as though they do defeats understanding at the start because it breaks the sequence of meaning. Readers and listeners gain no comprehension of the whole passage; they do better by seeing the whole meaning rather than bits and parts. The same considerations apply to the method of reading a verse, discussing it, then reading another verse, and so on.

Get acquainted in detail with the Bibles used by junior highs in your class. What difficulties do they present in format? Compare them with books the same pupils use in school. Locate the table or tables of contents. Compare abbreviations for the books given in them and those used in your teaching materials.

Compare a prose passage in a modern version of the Bible with the same passage in a Bible printed in verse-by-verse style (not always a matter of versions, as some editions of the King James Version are printed in paragraph style). Which is easier to read for meaning?

In order to see how these basics apply in class work, you are invited to guide part of a session with junior highs.

In our class each pupil brings his copy of the Bible. One pupil has left his home, however, so we lend him a copy from the class supply. We are at the point in the session at which we plan to read some Bible material. The teacher's outline suggested three brief passages, all related to one another. We divide the class into three work groups, forming the groups so that those sitting near each other work together. We call the attention of the junior highs to the three references that we wrote on the chalkboard before class time, and make sure that members of each group know which passage they are to look up. Or we might have written the references on slips of paper, one for each group.

Before the pupils start to look up the references, we say, "Here are some questions to be thinking about," and point again to the chalkboard. Alongside each reference we have written a question. Or we might have written them on the slips of paper given to the groups. Each group has a different question to think about.

While the young people find the references, we keep watch on how they do so. If one of them spends too much time leafing here and there, we remind him to use the table of contents in the front to find the book. We walk around, looking over shoulders, to be sure that each one has the right place. This may or may not be necessary, according to how much practice the junior highs have had in finding references.

Then we sit down among the pupils and read the Bible passages to ourselves while they read silently. It would be rude of us to sit staring into space or to bone up on our lesson. At the same time we are available to help if there is a question or a prolonged puzzled look. Either clue may mean that the pupil has found the wrong passage or come across a strange word. Or it may merely mean that he is thinking.

After the silent reading, the groups talk over what they have read. (How much time we allow for this depends on the difficulty of the material. If the meaning is fairly evident and answers to the questions are readily found, we may cut the group work rather short. We would then use the groupings chiefly in order to know to which pupils

we could turn in later discussion for information on a particular passage.) We work with each group in turn,
listening in on the discussion if it is going well. If discussion lags, we get it started by using the questions
assigned to the group or by asking members to tell in
their own words what was said in the Bible passage.
Perhaps we need to get a group back on the track by asking additional questions. In one group we spend time
trying to encourage the junior highs to think. They are
tending to rely on an answer made by one pupil. By asking
further questions we show them that there might be other
answers. Because of our encouragement, members of the
group offer ideas they had not expressed up to this time.

We find in our work with the groups that there is a
variety of answers in each one of them. Therefore we suggest that everyone be prepared to speak up in the discussion if he wants to. Sometimes we ask each group to
appoint one member who will lead off by reporting what
his group seemed to think.

When we see that each work group has discussed its
question and can probably go no farther, we call all the
junior highs into one large group again. We begin discussion by asking members of the first group to tell what
they read, what they talked over, how they answered
their question. We may question them further. Perhaps
we make some notes on the chalkboard or have a pupil
do so. Then we have the other two groups report in a
similar way.

We summarize briefly what the groups offered as answers to the questions, pointing out that there are many
different ideas and bringing the ideas together into a
question for further discussion.

Often the use of Bible material will look different from
the "reading in the light of a question" approach outlined
here. It may, for example, be part of the process of drama-
tizing a story or of constructing an interview of imaginary
eyewitnesses, or the like. The basic mechanics of the use

of the Bible remain much the same, whatever the method of approach. They are:

—Junior highs use Bibles in classwork.

—They learn to find different books by using the table of contents.

—They learn to read abbreviations and references by making frequent use of them, checking on their meaning when necessary.

—The references are before the pupils in writing, either on a chalkboard or on slips of paper or in the printed material (verbally given references should be rare).

—The pupils read silently for comprehension, each at his own pace.

—Usually they read with a question in mind or in terms of the use they will make of information in order to think further.

—Sometimes they have opportunity to talk over what they have read with a small group before talking it over with the entire class.

—Always there is time for individual or group thought and consideration before discussion in the class group.

—And always such Bible-reading leads toward the next step in the session—discussion or further consideration in some form or other.

Read again the part of a session "we" guided. You might number the basics listed above and locate each in the description (one is not illustrated).

What are the advantages of dividing into small work groups, having each take one of several passages? What disadvantages do you see to this way of working?

How would you describe the role of the teacher in guiding this kind of work?

FACT-FINDING IN BIBLE WORK

Beyond the more or less technical matters in the use of the Bible are other factors that have to do with learning to read, and that must be part of classwork. It is the teacher who first demonstrates the need for information, but each of these aspects of Bible study can be developed by the junior highs themselves in fact-finding work.

The Forming of the Bible. One need for information concerns the context of the Bible passage to be studied. If the Bible were one book like other books, or if every part were just like every other part (as is so often assumed to be the case), it would not be necessary to take context into account. As it is, the Bible is made up of many books of different types, dating from different times, composed in different ways and by different persons. Each of these facts contributes something to the nature and understanding of any passage that junior highs are to study.

The books of the Bible are different from books today in that almost none of them is the creative product of one writer. They are old books made up of even older strands of written and oral traditions. Few of them have authors we can identify. Some are attributed to other authors, in accord with a common practice of ancient times when there were no publishers, no royalties, and no copyrights. Almost no accounts were committed to writing within even a few decades of the events they record.

What all this means is that the teacher must have some knowledge of how the Bible was formed and an awareness of the differences among books. He must continually use such information in classwork. For example, the teacher can make it a practice to give a brief introduction to every Bible reference, using bits of information about a book. He does not need to tell everything or to make a lengthy introduction. Reading in a New Testament letter can be prefaced by the information that the writer was Paul, that the letter was addressed to the church at such a place (perhaps, also, which was having the problem of so-and-so), and was written probably so many years after Christ's death. As simple as it seems, it is always helpful if the introduction to a Bible passage tells whether it is poetry or a letter or history.

Another way to keep such information before junior highs is to display in the classroom a chart of the forming of the Bible. Casual but continual reference to it can help young people get a sense of the relation of books to events they tell about.

In addition to these rapid-exposure methods used by the teacher, there should be opportunity for the young people themselves to look up information on books of the Bible and on the forming of the Bible in general. For example, when a unit takes up several passages from Genesis, there should be one class member or a committee appointed to find out about the book of Genesis, how it came to be, why several stories are told more than once in it, and the like. Reports from the fact-finding should be given to the class and discussed in terms of how the information helps the pupils read with understanding.

Occasionally there will be, in the curriculum, units about the forming of the Bible. If continual work has been done along the way, such units can be more or less review.

Historical Background. A second kind of fact-finding relates to the historical nature of Bible material. Because time and place are important in almost all church school work, time lines and maps relating to current study ought to be regular parts of classroom decor. The teacher should learn to point pupils to them often by making casual reference when appropriate. Further historical background information is developed through activities outlined in the unit introduction and assigned to work groups. The methods of work are those outlined in the chapter on fact-finding.

However, a word of warning is in order. Many people think of Bible times as one blur of camels, pottery jars, and men in bathrobes. Actually, Bible times covered many centuries, and, as in all long periods of time, things changed over the years. Men of Abraham's time wore short tunics shaped somewhat like animal skins. Only centuries later did people of Bible lands take to wearing bathrobe-like garments (perhaps they didn't do so until churches started putting on plays about them). Camels were not always around, but came into use probably about the time of David. Even pottery didn't stay the same. It changed so much that remains of it are the major key used by archaeologists to date times and to designate cultures of Bible times. All of this is to suggest that if junior highs are going to search out and use the facts of Bible times, they need to be accurate rather than hazily romantic. The greater the amount and accuracy of background information, the more possible is identification between young people today and people of ancient times. Furthermore, junior highs have a passion for accuracy; they will be suspicious of attempts to put over on them an inaccurate romantic blur.

Words. A third kind of fact-finding necessary in study has to do with words and their meanings. If the Bible possessed some built-in magical principle by which all was immediately clear to the reader (and teachers often act as though it did), teacher and pupils would not need to bother with the meanings of words. But the Bible, like all reading matter, presents the reader with words to be understood, put together into phrases, sentences, paragraphs, all adding up to intelligent (i.e., requiring the intellect) meaning.

Some words that junior highs encounter in the Bible are more or less common, but new to their vocabularies. Other words denote objects or actions peculiar to other times and not known today, or different from objects and actions of today. For example, "king" and "war" have precise meanings in their historical contexts, different from what the words denote today. "Home," "spin," "tent," are other words that are not accurately understood if they call to mind only the things they mean today. Still other words have particular meanings in the vocabulary of faith, usually meanings that cannot be expressed in simple definitions. "Faith," "grace," "love," "sin," are examples of such words.

To initiate word study, the teacher might practice reading over beforehand all Bible material the junior highs are to use in a session, marking words that he thinks may cause difficulty. Sometimes they are indicated in the teaching plan, also. If there are only a few words, he might write them on the chalkboard. The definitions can be written after the words, or can be discussed in class and added to the list at that time. When there are a number of words, the teacher can make a poster on a large sheet of paper. Especially if the words recur in passages used in several sessions, the word list can be kept on display in the classroom.

The ways in which the teacher supplies word information should be only first steps, used to accustom the junior highs to the necessity for word study. As second steps, the teacher should plan ways to lead pupils toward looking up words on their own. For example, he can appoint a dictionary committee. If a Bible dictionary is available, the committee can be in charge of looking up needed words and reporting on them before the Bible-reading begins. Some word study, where it is concerned with customs, objects, and actions of Bible times, overlaps the work of finding out background information. The committee can make a word list for the unit and put it on the classroom wall, where junior highs can refer to it when they need to. Or the group can start to make a dictionary of their own that can be used by anyone in the class. Such a project is usually carried out over several units and is therefore passed to a new committee from time to time.

Look through your teaching materials for a unit of study centered in Bible material. What kind of information will the junior highs need about the Bible material, about time and place, about word meanings? What means are suggested in the unit resources for developing such information?

In order to see how these aspects of study are developed, you are invited to guide part of a session in a unit on the prophets of Old Testament times. The session takes up material from the prophet Isaiah.

The unit is well under way, so that our initial gathering and arrangement of resource materials was done several weeks ago. However, there are a few things we want to rearrange in the classroom and some materials we want to add for use especially in this session. When we enter the room we check over the resource materials to see that they are arranged invitingly. Among them are extra copies of the pupils' reading book, one of which we lay open at the chapter on Isaiah. We also have a Bible dictionary (belonging to the class) and a copy of *Everyday Life in Old Testament Times*, by E. W. Heaton (borrowed from the public library). For map work we have *The Westminster Historical Atlas to the Bible* and *Lands of the Bible* (A Golden Historical Atlas), by Samuel Terrien. Both of these have some text material that will be useful also. To call attention to the fact, we put a paper clip on the page of the *Westminster Historical Atlas* that has a chart of the history of Israel and the parallel histories of other nations of ancient times. Stapled in a colored paper folder we have an article from the December, 1960, *National Geographic*, "The Last 1000 Years Before Christ." Also on our table is a short filmstrip designed for use in a hand viewer, with a booklet that gives information about the pictures in the strip.

Especially for this session we have brought a picture of the prophet Isaiah that is one in a picture set about Old Testament times. We put this on an easel among the books on the resource table. We have also clipped some pictures from copies of the teacher's material: one of a statue labeled "Prophet" and another of a statue of Isaiah. We put these among the books.

On one wall of the classroom we have displayed side by side a time line of Bible history and a time line of the forming of the Bible, both from the picture set. These we have had on display since the beginning of this year of study and have referred to them often. Also from the picture set we have on display the map showing the two kingdoms of Israel and Judah.

Now we dismantle the bulletin board display we have used since the beginning of the unit. In its place we put up two questions written in large letters with felt-point

pen on a piece of white shelf paper. The questions are:
What do the headlines show about the kind of world we
live in today? What do they show about where we put our
trust as a nation? To emphasize the second question, we
have mounted a penny on another piece of paper and
printed "In God We Trust" alongside, with an arrow pointing to the words on the coin. Around these we put four
headlines about current wars, disarmament, weapons development—anything typical of the week just past. The
rest of the bulletin board we leave blank. On the resource
table we lay two newspapers we brought with us and a
pair of scissors.

In order to get ready for early arrivals, we arrange our
worktable in three sections. At each section we lay a copy
of the pupils' notebook open to the committee suggestions
for the unit. One of the pupils has made a sign for each
committee, by printing its name lengthwise on a folded
piece of drawing paper so that the sign stands on the table.
We put out these signs: "Chroniclers," "Map Changers,"
"Biographers." We also lay out for the Map Changers the
basic flannel map they have made for their work.

When the junior highs arrive, some of them bring headlines like the ones we have put on the bulletin board. We
talk briefly with each one about the headline, suggesting
that he add it to the bulletin board. A few, we find, have
not brought headlines. We suggest that they look through
the papers we brought and find some to add to the display.

In the meantime, other junior highs have started work
in the three committees. The Chroniclers are to find out
the main historical events of Isaiah's time, according to
some questions in the pupils' material. We work briefly
with the group to be sure the pupils know where to look
for facts. Some members of the committee start to review
the chapter in the reading book to find the needed information. To others we point out the chart in the *Westminster Historical Atlas*. To a rapid reader, we suggest
skimming *Lands of the Bible* (A Golden Historical Atlas).
We plan to return to work with these junior highs, be-

cause the information they are gathering is fairly complex. But for now, we leave them working on their own.

The Map Changers are to explain the time of Isaiah in terms of how the map changed. They need to look up some of the same information that the Chroniclers are finding. We suggest that they review the chapter in the reading book, then borrow the atlases from the other group. Or, perhaps, we suggest, the Chroniclers would give the Map Changers a brief report on what they have found out. Then the members of the group will need to assemble the cutouts to be used on the basic flannel map to show how it changed. They need to make some new cutouts also, such as a label for Jerusalem, where Isaiah preached.

The Biographers are to assemble information about the prophet himself. We have long ago learned that the members of this group do their basic work rather quickly and usually need extra work. Thus they have already absorbed everything in the reading book about Isaiah. We are prepared with some Bible references they can look up for more information. We also suggest that one member look up "Isaiah" in *The Westminster Dictionary of the Bible,* an adult book in the church library. Because the text is long, we warn him to skim it, looking for information about the prophet and skipping material about the book of Isaiah. We point out the three pictures of Isaiah, suggesting that the committee might pass them around as part of the report.

Next we go back to work with the Chroniclers again, especially to let them rehearse for us what they are going to present to the class. We suspect that our help may be needed in getting complicated details straight. On a sudden inspiration, we suggest that the Chroniclers and Map Changers work together, one group giving an oral report, the other illustrating it by adding to the map arrows to show invasions and by removing the Northern Kingdom to show its downfall.

When the three groups are ready, we suggest putting

work things aside, and call the attention of all the pupils to the bulletin board with its headlines. "What," we ask, "are the words or subjects that occur most often in headlines for this past week?" "War" will be one obvious answer, no matter what week it is. Then we ask, "As you read the news of this week, what kind of world did you find we live in?" (an obvious variation of the first question on the bulletin board). At this point we may need to take time to talk over in more detail some news items that especially interested the junior highs. We may need to listen to complaints about the sad mess the world is in, and the way adults have left the younger generation such a mess.

Soon we point out the coin and its motto, and ask the class whether the headlines bear out the motto. Then we bring up the second question on the bulletin board, talking it over only enough to hear whether the junior highs think we trust in God, or in something such as power, arms, or economic prosperity.

At this point we cut discussion of current times in order to make a transition to the past by saying: "Suppose we were talking over current news in Isaiah's time. What issues would we be discussing?" Instead of asking for spontaneous answers to the question, we use it to introduce the reports. The Chroniclers tell about times then, while the Map Changers illustrate on the flannel map. From the information they supply, we make a brief summary emphasizing the threat of invasion, the alliances made by Judah, the siege of Jerusalem that occurred during Isaiah's time. Then we ask the Biographers to tell others in the class about the prophet.

Next we have the junior highs turn to the notebook page for the session. It suggests press conferences with the prophet, outlines the procedure, gives the Bible references and some questions for both the interviewed and the interviewers. The material is divided into three parts, so we divide the class into three groups (not the same as the work groups). Together we read silently the general directions. We note that each group should have an Isaiah, while the others are to be reporters. In each case all are to study a Bible passage, a statement the prophet made. Then the reporters are to interview the prophet about his statement. Both prophet and reporters must know what is in the statement. The prophet must be ready to explain and, maybe, to defend his stand. The reporters will want to ask questions in terms of how the public will react to the prophet's statement. We point out that for two of the Bible passages, the material gives definitions of "words you will need to know." But, we say, if you find the prophet's words hard to understand, ask us and we will help you, or you can talk over the statement with others in your group.

Each junior high looks up the Bible passage for his group. We circulate among the pupils, seeing that each has found the place and making ourselves available to help with words or ideas that are difficult. When we are asked to help, we avoid as much as possible giving easy answers to the young people or doing their thinking for them. Instead, we point back to what the work groups have reported on, for much of the difficulty in understanding the prophet's words lies in having forgotten the specific historical problems of the time about which the prophet spoke.

When the groups begin to plan their press conferences on the basis of the Bible material, we circulate again. In two of the groups we suggest that all the reporters decide on one question they would like to ask the prophet. (This is a hasty adaptation we make because there seems to be some confusion in the groups, and we feel that they will be better off if each focuses on one thing). In the third group we find that the reporters have talked over possible questions. Each is ready to tackle the prophet. We work for a time with the prophets also, being sure they have grasped and can state the meaning of Isaiah's message. Although, strictly speaking, reporters and prophets should work separately—and some junior highs insist that they do —it is immaterial to us. If reporters and prophet wish to rehearse their unrehearsed press conference, it is all right.

We call the class together, introducing the reporters and the prophet for the first press conference. We suggest that the prophet start by giving the gist of his statement as found in the Bible passage assigned to that group (keeping in mind that others in the class have not read the passage). After he has done so, the reporters ask their questions. We have all three press conferences given in order. To summarize, we ask the pupils, "What were the main things Isaiah said about his time and about the people of God?" When a few of these have been mentioned, we ask, "How would the people of his time have reacted to Isaiah's ideas?" (essentially a review of the reporters' questions).

Next we introduce a thought question: "Why had the people turned from trusting in God to trusting in alliances and wars?" Over this question we spend a considerable amount of time, letting the young people suggest several answers and raise some questions of their own. From time to time, according to how the discussion goes, we add new questions. Our purpose throughout is to heighten the identification between young people in a warlike world today and God's people in a warlike world of yesterday. In addition, we want to help junior highs consider that both people, then and now, are under God, called, whether by a prophet or by his words studied later, to a basic trust in God.

Let us now look back and trace what we have done to help junior highs learn to read the Bible with understanding. We have:

—provided a place for study.

—equipped it with resources the junior highs can use.

—led up to and focused the first part of the session by a special assignment (from which we excused no one) and by use of the bulletin board display.

—guided the junior highs, through the committee work, in finding and sharing information about the past, without which the prophet's statements would not be comprehensible.

—explicitly helped junior highs identify themselves with people of the past by comparing our time and the time of the prophet.

—let the pupils read and consider some words of the prophet by a method—the press conferences—planned to focus their understanding in terms of the discussion and information used up to that point in the session.

—supplied needed words before the young people read.

—let the junior highs read the Bible material on their own while making ourselves available for help if needed.

—given them opportunity and motivation to think over on their own what they read in the Bible, by means of the point of view of prophet or reporter and the questions in the printed material.

—offered help in understanding through our supervision of the press conferences in preparation.

—summarized presentations of the Bible material by means of questions.

—moved on to a central thought question.

The work described here may seem somewhat elaborate, especially if it is new to you. Back of and prior to this episode, it is assumed, are: a teacher who is thoroughly prepared (see Chapter 6); an established atmosphere of work shared between teacher and pupils (see Chapter 7); pupils who are accustomed to working together in finding and sharing information (see Chapter 8).

Contrast the way of working described here with what is usually meant by teaching the Bible—for example, a talk by the teacher on Isaiah, reading the three Bible passages verse by verse around the class, discussing "what these verses mean to us." Consider: the role of the teacher, the amount of preparation needed, the amount of class time needed, what junior highs are expected to do, how much and what kind of learning might take place.

You may find it helpful now to review all of Chapter 4. Try to locate each of the basic methods described there in the session "we" guided. One is there by implication. One, "unbuilding," is not illustrated at all. It and the general method of thinking, considering, and weighing are developed in Chapter 10.

10. Considering

*How can the adult help young
adolescents think about, consider, and
weigh insights from the story of faith?*

EVERYBODY'S DOING IT

Everyone knows the answer to this question. It is
through discussion that the adult helps young adolescents
think, consider, and weigh.

Discussion has been the darling of youth work for many
years, so many years that most teachers today have a conditioned response to the word. Like Pavlov's dog that
learned to salivate when a bell rang, teachers of youth
have learned to stand and say, "Me too," at the sound of
the word "discussion." For example, when teachers are
asked to check a list of methods they use, everyone checks
"discussion."

However, questionnaires, in their tricky way, sometimes
include other types of questions that the teacher must
answer by describing what goes on in the class. Then it
appears that a variety of methods are called discussion.
Some teachers, who have been altogether brainwashed,
believe that discussion is the one appropriate way to work
with young people. To them, class equals discussion; they
use no other methods.

Teacher A gives a talk on faith, using examples from
the (better parts of the) life of David. Then he asks some
review questions, such as, "How did David use faith to be
a good king? How did he show that he wanted to worship
God?"

Teacher B has the pupils read in their Bibles the story of Saul's conversion. He then leads discussion of the following questions: "Was Saul a religious person? Was he a Pharisee? What was he going to do in Damascus? What happened to him on the way? Was he able to see afterward? Did he become a follower of Jesus? He was the greatest missionary in the early church, wasn't he?"

Teacher C brings to class a clipping from the newspaper. The "Dear Abby" column included a letter about a school bus that hit and killed a dog. The child who wrote to Abby was disturbed because the driver had not stopped. Several of the pupils have read the column also. So it is easy to get into discussion about death. The young people express many ideas about whether animals have souls and the possibility of an animal heaven, talk over funerals they have held for pets and some views on death. Into this chaos of ideas, the teacher tries to bring order with a short closing sermon on being kind to animals.

Teacher D, in reading through his material, notes that part of the session is to deal with "sin." He thinks it is a subject young people ought to discuss and one they have ideas about, and plans a discussion of sin for the class session. The discussion goes like this: "Today we are going to talk about sin. What is your idea of sin?" (Teacher's introduction and lead-off question.) "Doing something bad," "Disobeying your parents," "Disobeying God," "Swearing," "Killing," "Stealing," "Breaking the Ten Commandments," "Doing things that are against the law," "Not doing what your conscience tells you to do," are some ideas expressed by the pupils. "How does sin make you feel?" (Teacher's question.) "Bad," "Scared, because you know you'll be punished," "Sad," "Sorry," "Not as good as you thought it would make you feel," "Unhappy," say the junior highs. The teacher brings the discussion to a close by summarizing it: "We agree that sin is breaking God's laws and it makes you feel bad."

What each of these teachers knows with certainty is that as a good teacher of junior highs he ought to be using discussion. He has probably had plenty of guidance on the subject, for nothing is more tirelessly or thoroughly taken up in books, films, and training courses on youth work. Thus the teacher who cannot wean himself away from a lecture makes a halfhearted attempt at discussion following it. And the one who cannot stop using the Bible as knowledge lets the young people express themselves by means of a few obvious questions. Both of these teachers could explain the importance of allowing junior highs an opportunity to speak. The other two teachers are also enthusiastic about having the pupils express their ideas, perhaps because their versions of discussion require so little preparation on the part of the teacher.

Some of these common uses of discussion have validity in their proper places. Review of factual information has its place. Letting young people express themselves is important. Finding out what the group thinks can be valuable also. But discussion used in the process of study to help young adolescents think, consider, and weigh takes on rather different dimensions.

What does discussion mean to you?
Analyze the procedures of the four teachers. Were they using discussion? If so, how would you characterize the type of discussion each used? Do you regard the questions they used as thought-provoking or thought-stopping? Imagine how junior highs in each of these classes might react to the discussion. Would they find it challenging or boring? engaging their participation or leaving them cold?

The rest of this chapter deals with discussion in the process of thinking, considering, and weighing as part of study. Discussion has other uses in classwork, suggested or illustrated in the following places:

Conversation—demonstration session in Chapter 7 (with individual pupil in relation to a display); demonstration session in Chapter 8 (committee work).

Planning—demonstration session in Chapter 7, see especially the section "One Last Question."

Using audio-visual material—the section "Audio-Visuals: Ooh! and Ugh!" in Chapter 8.

Reading the Bible—second demonstration session in Chapter 9. Part of the discussion is of the review-of-information type.

Reporting—see "Report from a Committee" and guidelines for the teacher in Chapter 8.

In order to consider how discussion is used in study, you are invited to share in guiding parts of several sessions. The first of these episodes takes up the story used to illustrate general methods in Chapter 4. The second and third episodes continue sessions started in Chapters 8 and 9.

THE STORY OF JOSEPH

The junior highs have been exploring the story of Joseph. Because the story is too long for reading, we divided the class into three groups. Each group was responsible for reading part of the story and planning around it one act of a three-act play. An outline of the story helped each group see how its act was part of the whole story. When the three acts of the drama were presented, it was clear to both actors and audience that the climax of the story occurred in the scene in which Joseph and the brothers were reconciled.

In order to focus on this point we ask the pupils what other kinds of ending the story might have had. What would they have done if they had been Joseph? "He might," we suggest, "have had his brothers thrown into jail for attempted murder." "Or sued them for $10,000," one of the junior highs picks up our imaginative lead. But another pupil sees that this would not have been likely in ancient times. "No, but he could have demanded that they be his slaves for life." "He could have said, 'See? Dreams come true,'" says one of the young people. "Huh?" is the reaction of both the pupils and us. "What do you mean?" we ask. "Well, he dreamed they would all bow down to him, and they did." The idea begins to make sense, and someone else says, "So he could have lorded it over them as he'd always wanted to do." "Or, at least, he wanted to do that when he was young," we add, just to keep things accurate.

"What *did* he say and do?" we ask. Then we suggest,

"Look up the references." We point to two references in Genesis listed on the chalkboard. "These are two different tellings of the story. Contrast what is said in them with the possibilities we've been suggesting." This is a thought question intended to help the junior highs in reading; we don't plan to develop it in discussion, although we might if any of the pupils chose to express his ideas on it.

After everyone has had a chance to read, we ask, "How did God use the imperfect character of Joseph and the murderous actions of his brothers to carry out the purposes he had for this family?" The question is chiefly for review. Its literal answer—that it was possible for them to get food while others suffered famine—is mentioned by a member of the class. Another pupil starts to say he thinks there is more to the story than that—the brothers came together as a family again. But he is interrupted by still another pupil on whom the meaning of the question has just dawned. "Couldn't God have carried out his purposes better through good people?" We ask this boy to explain more of what he is thinking. He has difficulty doing so. The best he can come up with is, "If Joseph hadn't been so conceited and the brothers hadn't been so jealous, they could all have stayed home and worked the farm together. Then they would have had food." His last point gets demolished by the others on the grounds that a famine is a famine, no matter how good you are at farming.

Before the class embarks on an agricultural discussion, we cut in, suggesting that we can't change the story, but had better look at it as it is. "A good point has been raised," we say, "in the question of whether God couldn't have done better working through good people from the beginning." We review the ancestors of Joseph—Abraham and Jacob, for example, who, as we saw in previous explorations, were not exactly good people either. We point out that many people would agree with what the questioner is suggesting, because they think, If I were God, I would choose good people to carry out my purposes.

"But he did choose a good person, finally, in Jesus

Christ," offers a pupil. "That's how we think of him. Did people in his time consider him good?" we ask. "Yes," say many of the pupils. "*Some* people did," say a few. "Did the good people of his time think he was good?" we ask. "Well, no," say several pupils.

Two possibilities are beginning to occur to the young minds around us. Maybe "good" is not so settled as we always thought, many are thinking. And at least one young person is about to turn it all around, just as Paul said people did in his time, and say, "Let's sin so that good can come of it."

We ask casually: "Do you think you can divide people into the goodies and the baddies? What about the objectionable things in the characters of Joseph and his brothers —are they typical of bad people?" "I'm like that," confesses one member of the class, and then is scared by his own honesty, "—sometimes. Everyone's that way sometimes." "Yeah," agree several others. "But God doesn't want us to be that way," says a girl.

"What does he do about it?" we ask. "He punishes you," the girl replies with certainty. "How?" asks a less certain pupil. "Well, you get unhappy, or you have troubles." (This idea is regularly brought out in class discussion and just as regularly questioned by the pupils.) "Only," points out another pupil, "in this story that didn't happen." We were just going to say something of the sort ourselves in order to bring out the contrasting insight from the story. Now that it is pointed out, we let the other pupils react to it.

MEMBERS OF THE CHURCH IN THE MIDDLE AGES

The junior highs are taking the parts of medieval people. They have studied descriptions of themselves and listened to a report from the committee on everyday life, and each has introduced himself, telling about his occupation and how he lives. Singling out a servant girl who works in the castle and a priest, we questioned the pupils about the differences between these two.

In exploring the differences between clergy and laity, we began to see that "church" in medieval times meant the system of clergy and their power over the people. We asked what kind of power the clergy had. Because the junior highs were vague about this, we reviewed information about the belief in purgatory and in the power of priests over forgiveness.

Next we asked the pupils to look at Matt. 16:18–19, explaining the use of these verses to support belief in the power of the clergy to forgive sins. Together we looked back to establish the context of the verses. We decided that, as a story, the passage tells about Peter's confession of faith in Jesus Christ, but that separate verses taken out of it might be used to mean other things.

Against this background of information, identification, and Bible interpretation, we ask, "Do you think that medieval people liked or resented the fact that the priests had so much power over them?" Almost everyone in the class seems to think that people must have resented it. "Why do you think so?" we ask. Everyone wants to be free, is the general meaning of the answer contributed by several members of the class. "Is that true?" we ask; no one answers.

So we say, "People then lived under the shadow of a great fear, the fear of eternal punishment. They believed the priests had the only means of escaping or lessening that punishment. Suppose you lived under such a threat. Wouldn't you depend on the people who could show you a way out?" "Yes, but you wouldn't want to." "You'd *want* to be free, even if you couldn't." "You might want to rise up and overthrow the clergy sometime." "But people didn't," we point out. "You might do things secretly against them," suggests a pupil. "And many people did, although they were often put down by the powerful organization of the clergy," we add for information.

"I suspect that people mostly liked the fact that the priests had so much power over them," we say, and then ask, "Is it entirely true to say that people want to be free?"

The question still baffles the young people, so we ask, "What about you? Do you ever want someone to tell you what to do?" It is beginning to occur to many that they really do want to be told what to do—by their parents, for example.

We turn the question to matters of faith. "We often say that God asks us to obey his will. Do you sometimes wish someone would come right out and say exactly what his will is and what you should do?" In such a form, the possibility has appeal. "That's right," says one boy. "They're always saying you should do what God wants you to do, but no one ever says what that is." "Or tells you how to find out," adds another pupil. "That's what the Bible is for; it tells you what God wants you to do." "But . . . ," begins a girl, hesitating to cast doubt on the Bible. However, one of the boys is not so hesitant and says, "No, it doesn't, really. It doesn't tell me what to do in school or what kind of career I should plan." "You know what I mean," says the pupil who thinks the Bible tells people what to do. The two are on the verge of an argument.

"Why is it," we ask, "that no one tells you exactly what God wants you to do? Is it because all of us adults just don't know, or want to make you figure it out for yourselves, or what?" "I guess they want us to figure it out for ourselves." "Maybe they don't know either. I mean, maybe that's not because they are ignorant, but maybe they're supposed to figure it out for themselves too."

"How would you feel if someone took charge of your faith, told you what to do and believe, as priests in medieval times did?" we ask. "But that wasn't faith!" blurts out one pupil. "What do you mean?" we ask. He is, after all, not too sure. Another pupil says, "That way, what you mostly believe in is the priest, not God."

"In other words," we add, "you'd be relying on the authority of another person. Would the same thing be true today if someone gave you authoritative guidance about what God wants you to do?" "Not if it was really

God's will," answers a pupil. "How would you know?" asks another. "Just because somebody said he knew for sure?" "What about that?" we add. "People in medieval times were taught that God willed for them eternal punishment and wanted them to spend a lifetime working their way out of it. Looking back, we think that kind of faith was based on fear and enforced by authority." "You mean, if someone today told us what to believe and do, he might be wrong too?" The question is directed to us, but before we can answer another pupil says, "Or he might want power over us." We cannot resist adding, though we think only a few pupils will understand, "If you want someone to do something, it's a very good thing to have God behind you." Then we realize this went home more than we had anticipated; most of the young people can recall times when parents and others have used God to back up their own authority.

The session is drawing to a close, so we say, "Here's something to think about. Remember the Bible passage we looked at? In the medieval church those verses were used to support authority. When we studied them, it seemed to us they said more about faith than about authority. What's the difference between authority and faith? What's the difference between an enforced system of belief or behavior, and faith? Think it over. We'll talk about it again next week."

THE PROPHET ISAIAH'S MESSAGE

In this session we are studying some passages from Isaiah. The junior highs have worked in three committees to find out what was happening in the prophet's time, where events took place, and information about the prophet.

We talked over some headlines from current newspapers to see what events were characteristic of our own day. Then we looked back to Isaiah's time by hearing reports from the committees, and considered how the prophet's time was also one characterized by war, alliances, and defense measures.

The pupils looked up some things the prophet said in the midst of such a time. The results of their study were presented as press conferences, with reporters asking the prophet what he meant and how people would react to his ideas. Reviewing the prophet's statements, we found that he was critical of alliances that the nation of Judah was making; that, unlike other spokesmen and leaders, the prophet did not believe in saying, "Everything is all right"; that he criticized the people of God for relying on armaments.

Next we ask, "Why had the people turned from trusting in God to trusting in alliances and war?" "They were afraid," say several junior highs. "They *had* to," says another emphatically. We ask this pupil to explain his idea. "Well, if those bigger, more powerful nations were going to overrun them, they had to protect themselves." "Yes," chime in others, "they couldn't just sit there and let the Assyrians walk in." There follow several different expressions of the idea that the best defense is a good offense. Opinion rapidly swings toward the view that trusting in arms and alliances is the realistic way to live in a warlike world.

We cut in to say, "You sound just like the people to whom Isaiah spoke. I can imagine that they expressed exactly the ideas you are expressing. They were scared. They had to protect themselves. They had to let their enemies know that they would fight and not stand for invasion. They had to be practical. The prophet Isaiah made a serious accusation of God's people precisely because they thought these things. I guess you think the prophet's message from God was very unrealistic."

Everyone hesitates. Clearly, God's message through his spokesman ought to mean something, but it does not seem to make good sense. Finally a pupil says hesitantly, "Did God really want them to do nothing and let the enemy

walk over them?" "That's what Jesus said about 'turning
the other cheek,' isn't it?" asks someone. The question is
directed to us, so we say, "Is it?"

The parallels with our own time are too obvious to be
kept out of the discussion. One pupil asks, "Does that
mean that we should just let the Communists take over the
world and bomb us first?" The other pupils are undecided
as to whether this is what it might mean. "To whom was
the prophet speaking?" we ask. "The people of God," the
pupils answer. "Is the United States today the people of
God?" "Yes" and "No" are the answers. We know from
previous discussions that it is difficult for these young
people to admit that Americans are not the people of God
and to refrain from making simple applications of the
Bible.

"What was the real issue for God's people in Isaiah's
time, according to the prophet?" we ask, trying to get the
discussion back on focus. A pupil identifies this for us
again as the question of where they were putting their
trust. "Which is easier to do, to trust God, who can't be
seen, or to trust in armaments, which can be seen?" The
answer is obvious, so we point out that the people were
really taking the easy way out. The comment provokes
a number of "Yes, but's . . ."

"It seems," we add, "that your comments—which we
said were rather like those of people in Isaiah's time—
show that the people were chiefly interested in saving
their nation. Perhaps the prophet meant to point out to
them that such a goal was not a proper one for God's
people. In other words, saving themselves was not what
they were supposed to do as God's people. Yet they un-
doubtedly felt, as you do, that they could serve God better
by being a strong nation rather than taking the risk of
being conquered."

In our summary we have attempted to point out the
inescapable contrast between the will of the people and
the will of God. Nobody is satisfied. We are well aware

that many of the junior highs are still saying, "Yes, but, . . ." as they leave. It is clear that being a strong nation wins hands down against the prophet's views of how the people of God are to trust him. But something of the prophet's message and a glimmering of how God's way is usually different from ours—we think these things have at least been heard and may be food for thought.

THE DISCIPLES OF JESUS

The session started with a question we wrote on the chalkboard: "If you had a very important message to give to everyone in the world, how would you go about making it known?" We asked each junior high as he arrived to think of some answers, but we saved discussion of the question for a later time.

We divided the class into three groups each to prepare a reading of a passage in John, ch. 1. The passages record conversations between Jesus and men whom he called to be his disciples. The pupils made signs for themselves: "The Gospel Writer," "John the Baptist," "A Disciple of John," "Jesus," and the like. They practiced reading their parts from the Bible, the Gospel Writer reading the verses that are not dialogue. When they finished this work, each group presented its conversation.

Next we talked over three review questions about the conversations: "How are they all related to one another? What did Jesus tell these men about their futures? What different titles for Jesus Christ are used?"

Then we turn to the question on the chalkboard. The junior highs have several different ideas for making an important message known to everyone. They favor TV, radio, and newspapers as obvious ways to reach many people, although one pupil points out that there are people in the world who would not be reached by any of these.

We ask, "How did Jesus go about making known the message he brought to the world?" "By preaching," answer a number of pupils. "And teaching," adds another. Then

a pupil who remembers the Bible study senses that Jesus'
main method was by gathering a small group of followers.
To reinforce the point, we remind the pupils that most of
those who heard Jesus speak deserted him, even though
they were attracted to him for a time. After his death and
resurrection, the men who made him known were the
disciples who had been with him.

"Suppose Jesus had had our modern means of communication available. Do you think he would have used them
instead of this method of getting a few followers?" "I think
he would have used every means he could to tell people
about God," answers a boy. "But TV's not so hot," says a
girl. "I mean, people can always turn it off if they don't
want to see what's on. Or they could have looked at him
and thought, 'He's just a crackpot.' " "Which is more or less
what Jesus' brothers thought of him," we add. "Some of
those preachers on the radio are crackpots, all right!" says
one pupil.

"Were you suggesting that Jesus might not have used
TV?" We refer the question to the girl who said TV was
not so hot. "Well, I meant maybe it wouldn't have been as
good as choosing disciples. I mean, even if he'd gone on
TV, he would have had to have disciples anyhow." Several
in the class agree with this. "Why?" asks a boy who seems
to be intrigued still by the possibility of Jesus on TV. "It's
different, somehow," says the girl. Before we can ask her
to explain why, another pupil starts to explain, "You don't
really get to know someone on TV or in a newspaper
article."

"You learn about things or ideas or events, and you get
impressions of people, but you don't get to know them
face-to-face," we rephrase his idea. "I think Jesus wanted
his followers to live with him and know him," adds a pupil.
"He didn't so much have a message—I mean, he was the
message," says another. To carry the idea farther, we ask,
"How would it be if the members of your family never
saw one another but communicated only by two-way radio

or TV?" A few pupils laugh. "Like science fiction," comes an unexpected answer. We are not up on science fiction, so we have to have explained to us some of the communications devices being used in the future of fantasy. The illustrations the pupil uses are somewhat obscure, but to the point, because he has sensed the lack of personal relationship in them.

Then we introduce a new question, building on the former discussion: "This kind of firsthand knowing we talked about between Jesus and his disciples—is that possible for followers of Christ today?" We search out the pupil who lingered long with the imaginary Jesus on TV, because we wonder if this wasn't the question at the back of his mind. Perhaps he was protesting, as we have heard others in the class do, "If only I could see, I would believe."

PAUL'S DISCOVERY

The unit is about the new people of God in New Testament times and takes up passages from The Acts and some of the letters of Paul. We started the session with a question: "What do you think is the most important matter for a person to face up to when he has become a member of the church?" "How to obey God," was the answer generally agreed on, although it was expressed in different ways.

Next we asked two pupils to carry out an unrehearsed conversation with us. They took the parts of members of the church talking to a nonmember who asked what he must do to be a Christian. The conversation brought out more ideas on the problem of how to obey God. Most of the ideas included being good or living up to moral standards.

To explore the matter further, the junior highs studied Phil. 3:4–11, verses in which Paul explained why he had discarded all his old righteousness—the righteousness of being and doing right—for a new kind of relationship with

God in Christ. The study took considerable time because we worked carefully with the meanings of words and phrases. To sum up, we talked over where Paul had formerly put his confidence and where he indicated he would put his confidence from then on. We used an illustration of two kinds of families: one in which a person is a good member because he follows the family rules; another in which a person is a good member because he is a member.

Then we raise a question that has come up often in classwork. "When you become a member of the church, would you rather be given a set of rules or the opportunity to know a living Savior?" The question always stirs a certain amount of discontent among the junior highs. There are some who really would like more guidance in the form of rules or standards. There are others who value the possibility of working it out for themselves. A new idea comes up in the discussion today.

"They do give you a set of rules!" says one pupil strongly. "They didn't give me any!" counters another. "Yes, they did," says the first one, "they just didn't write it down one-two-three. But they sure do expect you to be a certain kind of person and do certain things. You try not doing them and see what happens. You break the law, and they aren't likely to call you 'member of the church' anymore; they're going to call you 'j.d.' "

It is a long and somewhat bitter statement. We do not know what personal feelings underlie it. But we know that it is possible for the boy to make such a statement because of the kind of discussion we have had in the class. Also the current unit of study has given the young people a means of being critical of the church as it is. The "church as it is" the junior highs always refer to as "they," meaning the adults, a realistic recognition of the power structure in which the young people have little part. It has not occurred to them that they too are the church.

Some junior highs in the class agree with the idea of rules that are not written down one-two-three. Others are baffled by the subtlety of the point. So we say: "Suppose the rules were listed one-two-three. For example, suppose each Sunday in church we recited, 'On my faith, I will try to do my duty to God and my country . . .'" We continue, imitating the Scout purpose and rules. Comments come thick and fast now. Some pupils recall the discussion last week about membership in the church, in which we talked about the difference between loyalty to an organization and loyalty to a person. They see that there could be something inappropriate in the set of standards. Others recall the Bible study and the discussion of where Paul put his confidence. They suspect that rules would lead to putting confidence in one's ability to keep them, the very attitude that Paul discarded.

"Let's try another spontaneous conversation," we suggest. We call on two pupils (not the same ones who took part in the previous conversation) to be church members talking to a nonmember about what he must do to be a Christian. The pupils who did this earlier, we point out, used merely their own ideas. These pupils are to try to express what they have learned in study today.

They explain to us, the inquiring nonmember, that being a Christian is having faith in Christ. They tell us some things it is not: for instance, not belonging to an organization, or not living up to a set of rules. We cut in after a few minutes, dropping our role in the conversation, and ask others in the class what they might have said to us. Their ideas also add up to what being a Christian is not.

We point out this fact and, dropping back into our role of nonmember again, say, "As one who never belonged to a church, I had the impression that Christians were supposed to be the good people of the world setting an example for the rest of us. Now you tell me it isn't that way. It sounds to me as though you are saying that Christians and everyone else are free to do anything they want to."

There is a moment of panic in which almost every pupil says, "No, that's not true!" "All right," we say, "what are we supposed to do?"

Because the question is followed with silence, we go to the chalkboard and begin to make some notes on the class discussion up to this point, talking about them as we write. Our summary goes like this: "Paul's discovery: old righteousness out, replaced by confidence in Christ. We think: rules might be O.K.; it's better to figure out things for yourself; there really are rules even though it doesn't seem so. Rules might make it like an organization instead of faith, or might mean putting confidence in ourselves instead of in Christ."

"But," we continue, "we seem to think that the opposite of having and keeping rules is doing anything you please. Do you think that is what Paul did?" Nobody thinks he did just anything, but no one is sure what he did. "Could it be that 'keeping the rules' has another opposite besides 'doing anything?'" We take a brief excursion to show that many words have more than one opposite. The opposite of "empty," for example, might be "full" or "half full."

"Here is a situation," we say, "that might have come about in our church. In this situation church members could decide to use their energy one way or another. One way means they would be investing their energy in concern with themselves and their own goodness. See if you can decide what the other way represents."

We then tell about a church that hears a bar is to be opened on the corner near it. One of the members feels that a committee should be formed to keep a bar from opening so near the church, because it would lower the character of the neighborhood. On the same day an officer of Alcoholics Anonymous calls the church office to ask if a new chapter could meet Saturday evenings in the church. If they did, arrangements for church school could not be completed on Saturday by the custodian, but would have to be made early Sunday morning by the teachers or by a special committee.

There is not time to discuss the situation fully. Most of the junior highs see that wanting to keep the bar out of the church neighborhood represents mostly concern for the church's own righteousness. One young person tries to suggest that if they kept the bar out, then they wouldn't have to have the AA meeting, but the others know this is unrealistic. Nobody is certain what, in this situation, you would call the opposite of "keeping the rules" and concern with one's own goodness. So we suggest that the junior highs think of a name for it during the coming week.

Reread these examples of discussion, looking especially for the following in each: Other methods used in the session; what preceded discussion; the role of the teacher; the kinds of questions used; what seems to be the aim.

The questions used were taken from curriculum outlines. Look through your teaching materials for methods and questions directed toward thinking, considering, and weighing. Study in detail one suggested plan for discussion. What question or questions are suggested? What different ideas might junior highs express in response to one of them? Consider several possibilities. If they said, "thus and so," what would you say or ask next? Or if they said, "that," what would you ask? Suppose some said, "thus and so," while others said, "that." (This is how teachers prepare for discussion in classwork.)

In the following analyses of discussion, examples are used from demonstration discussions. Keep a finger or a marker in the preceding pages while you read the next sections.

WHERE DISCUSSION STARTS

In study, discussion starts from somewhere, the somewhere being a part of the story of faith. Discussion is, therefore, not the only method used. It grows out of prior work, out of identification, information, insight, and the pupils' ideas.

Teacher D (in the episodes at the beginning of the chapter), by contrast, starts from nowhere. The discussion of sin he leads is informed only by the pupils' ideas. Teacher C, who brings to class an account of the death of a dog, starts from "what the junior highs are interested in," which is also, essentially, nowhere.

In all the demonstration sessions, the junior highs have opportunity before discussing to get acquainted with part of the story of faith—either Bible material or an episode from church history. What they learned in such work was used in discussion.

Part of what the junior highs bring to the discussion is their *identification* with persons and incidents in the basic material. Sometimes, as in taking up the story of Joseph, the identification is developed further in the discussion. In another session, the pupils take the parts of medieval people in order to imagine what it was like to be members of the church then. Identification is suggested by means of an initial question in taking up Paul's discovery about faith and righteousness. Beyond these specific examples is the broader background of identification, the "living into" the story which each young person experienced, if the basic material was well developed.

Fact-finding is used also to help the pupils discuss on the basis of information, rather than from nowhere. In imagining themselves as medieval people, the junior highs use background information presented by committees. They rely on facts about the prophet and his time in discussing Isaiah's message. Such information is used to further identification, as well as to interpret Bible material in its context of time and place.

Insight, or "seeing into" the basic material in terms of the *God - man* relationship, often shapes the central question taken up in discussion. The dramatic high point of the Joseph story, the reconciliation of the brothers and Joseph's explanation, leads to the question of how God used actions that were meant to be evil. Pretending to be medieval people leads to thinking about the relationship between laity and clergy and about the nature of faith in such a relationship. Studying the message of Isaiah in a time of war and the reaction of people to it leads to considering what kind of trust God asked from his people. Discussing the calling of Jesus' disciples leads to questions about the difference between making a message known and the way Jesus Christ made God known. These questions, in turn, lead to thinking about whether faith today can be a personal relationship. Considering the discovery Paul made about the worthlessness of his righteousness leads to discussion of what Christians are to do.

Each of these insights represents the main identification in the basic material. Each is made up of specifics—people, time, place, actions, feelings. Discussion picks up and develops the insight in terms of the specifics of then, and in doing so, touches on the specifics of now in the lives of young adolescents.

The point is worth emphasizing, because many teachers are tempted to be general rather than specific. It seems easier, especially if discussion is the favored method, to read through a lesson plan, select the questions for discussion, and let the junior highs discuss them (the procedure of Teacher D in the episodes at the beginning of the chapter). From material about Paul's discovery, the teacher who works this way would choose for class discussion the question of what Christians should do. To such a discussion, the young people bring ideas uninformed by anything other than their own thoughts and experiences, and what they have been taught. By pooling their ideas, they will come to the conclusion that Christians are to be good. That is what they very likely think, what they experience in their church, and what they have been taught. The insight from the story of faith, which the teacher has not bothered to help the pupils see, calls such an idea into question. Most junior highs dimly sense that they are being cheated out of something when they are asked to rehearse nothing more than their own opinions.

There is, also, a tradition in church school work that tempts the teacher to be general. It is the tradition of the lesson, the principle to be extracted from the Bible, and learned and applied by the pupils. The teacher who yields to this temptation will make use of the Bible material, but he will move quickly from it to the general principle or to a general question. Several of the demonstration discussions deal with aspects of faith. In many of them the teacher could have moved from the basic material to the general question "What is faith?" But in each case, faith was to be considered in a specific way—for example, from within the situation of people under authority, or from the position of a man faced with the question of what his righteousness is worth. Such specifics find echoes in the experiences and thoughts of junior highs, that is, identification. The abstract theme, principle, or concept does not. It has to be forced on the pupil's mind. Usually the concept to be learned is beyond the young person's level of thinking, because he has not yet known enough specifics from which to form the concept. Thus, for a second reason, the lesson has to be forced. Once in the pupil's mind, the assumption goes, it can and will be applied. Junior highs tend to be bored with such teaching because it goes right past them; it finds no lodging place within them.

Often the quickly-arrived-at generality is an "ought" or "ought not," that is, a moral. The teacher who is tempted to proceed from Bible material to a lesson in character development will experience some difficulties if he approaches the Bible with any openness of mind. It does not deal with moral examples and moral lessons. However, usually such a teacher has a closed frame of reference for the Bible. When he comes across studies in Bible material that do not support a clear moral, he ignores them, substituting something that does. The moral generality stops thinking. Who thinks when he is ordered to do this or do that? But it only seems as though the one who receives orders is not thinking. He may well be thinking underground. That is how young people react to being told what to do. They continue thinking—but inside, usually in whatever term is now equivalent to "Nuts!" The teacher loses touch with the thoughts of the pupils. Indeed, he could not bear to hear what they are thinking.

What the junior highs think plays an important but distinct part in discussion as used in study. Most young

people can see and identify the central insight or meaning
of a story. For example, the pupils who prepare press conferences with the prophet Isaiah understand what he said
and what the people of God then wanted to think and do.
At the same time, the young people hold opinions quite
at variance with the insight they have gained. They cling
to a thoroughly practical, up-to-date conviction about
defense in a warlike world.

This is the point at which the pupils' ideas are brought
into discussion, the point of contrast with the central
insight of faith. It is of some importance to develop how
the young people feel and what they think, and of equal
importance to hold before them the insight they have
gained.

To many teachers it seems easier and entirely possible
simply to teach the insight as a new learning. To do so is
to waste effort, if young people are inwardly thinking,
"That's crazy," or "Nonsense," or "It's impossible." They
can and will vote for their own opinions, which remain
entirely unruffled by the new insight.

What study is all about is the ruffling of whatever ideas
junior highs currently hold. Insights from the story of
faith never make sense; they are always nonsense and
impossible. The teacher deliberately puts them over
against present thoughts so that "what we now think" can
be examined in a new light. Junior highs do not examine
and question their present thoughts by the enforcement of
a new learning, parroted back to the teacher, and repeated
until it is mastered. They do so by expressing what they
now think, by bringing their ideas from the background
of thinking out into the open where they can be looked
at. The essential difference about discussion in study lies
in this contrasting function, which is not developed when
discussion is undertaken because self-expression is good
for young people or in order to come to a group decision.

The way of contrast is seldom easy; it can be intricate.
It is not easy in the discussion of Isaiah. The insight from
faith is constantly outweighed by the convictions of the

young people. The discussion of medieval people becomes intricate. At first the pupils firmly believe that anyone would rebel against authority. They do so out of their convictions about freedom. The teacher presses the point by using historical facts, and then by putting the question in terms of how the young people feel. The conviction about freedom turns out to be a generality, not well supported by the realization that they (and others) do want to be told what to do. Then the contrast between faith and authority can be suggested.

From dramatization of the story of Joseph, the junior highs see and grasp the insight that God may make good of actions intended to be evil. But one pupil candidly expresses his feeling that God might have done better with good persons to work with. His idea leads to the question of who is good and whether the young people themselves are not more or less like Joseph and his brothers.

The study of Paul's discovery puts his insight over against a common idea that Christians are to strive for goodness. The junior highs recognize this common idea in an imaginary conversation with a nonmember of the church. They also recognize it in their own wishes for more definite guidance in being members of the church. In a more subtle sense, they recognize it in one pupil's feeling that church members are forced to conform, although not openly. Then they have to reckon with the fact that Paul's view of the matter is quite different from the common idea.

In all these discussions, the teacher can neither leave the junior highs comfortable with their own ideas nor enforce the new insight. His concern is with the confrontation between these two—present ideas versus insights from the story of faith. It is here that young adolescents begin thinking about, considering, and weighing insights from the story of faith. This is the heart of discussion in study.

To trace further how discussion proceeds from prior work, turn back and read: (1) the demonstration session in Chapter 8, followed by the demonstration discussion of faith in medieval times and (2) the second demonstration session in Chapter 9, followed by the demonstration discussion of Isaiah's message. These readings represent two complete sessions of work with junior highs.

Try explaining in your own words the differences between: discussion that starts nowhere and discussion that grows out of prior work; discussion that deals in generalities (a lesson or principle) and discussion that deals in specifics; discussion that enforces a new learning and discussion that focuses on contrast.

What difficulties do you see in the view that the heart of discussion in study is "present ideas versus insights from the story of faith"? Does it raise questions about the abilities of young adolescents, time, methods, the outcome of discussion?

What is meant by the statement that insights from the story of faith are always nonsense and impossible? Do you agree or disagree with the statement?

How Discussion Goes

Questions are what the teacher uses to get discussion started and to keep it going. But much depends on the kind of question the teacher asks. Equally much depends on the kind of answer he expects and how he handles the answers made by the pupils.

The simplest use of questions is for recitation. The teacher asks questions that have definite answers found in the basic material studied. Some answers are right; some are wrong. Teachers A and B, in the episodes at the beginning of the chapter, use such questions exclusively. In the discussion of Jesus' disciples, recitation is used briefly to review the Bible passages read.

Review questions are used for comprehension. If study were aimed at comprehension of the basic material (if its aim were "knowing the Bible"), then recitation would be the main method. It is all right to proceed as Teachers A and B do, using nothing but recitation, and discussion of Jesus' disciples stops at review of the facts in the Bible material. But comprehension is only one step in study, one of the bases for the further work of thinking, considering, and weighing. Thus recitation plays a minor, preparatory part in discussion.

When the teacher wishes to help young people move toward thinking, considering, and weighing, he must choose questions that stimulate thought. They are questions that go beyond information to meaning. They do not have correct answers. The right answers are thoughtful ones; the only wrong answers are those that do not aid thoughtfulness.

The *initial question,* or questions, is usually planned around the main identification point, that is, the insight the pupils have gained from the source material. Discussion of the Joseph story starts with the pupils using their imaginations and suggesting what they would have done. Junior highs are asked to express their ideas of how medieval people felt about the church's authority. "Do you think . . . ?" the lead-off question begins. Because it can be answered with a simple yes or no, it is followed quickly by, "Why do you think so?" The initial question in studying Isaiah's message asks the why of the things that have been learned about prophet and people. Discussion of Jesus' disciples and of Paul's discovery both start with a question suggested at the beginning of class time and cast in terms of what the pupils think.

What kinds of answers will be made to such questions? Since the questions are intended to elicit opinions, expressions of opinion are what the teacher should get. Very often he does not, because of the young people's previous experience and also because of his own expectations. For example, the pupils may be accustomed to recitation. When a question is asked, they search in their minds for the right answer, hesitate to answer unless they think they are right, begin waving hands to attract the teacher's attention, and address their answers directly to the teacher. Other pupils, who long ago learned that they never have the right answers, sit on the sidelines, disinterested and often resentful. The teacher who expects such a process to take place sets an atmosphere in which it does. He looks for the pupil with the right answer, by selecting one of the hands waving in his face or by knowing which pupils are usually right and therefore safe to call on. He listens to the answer, discards it if it is wrong, accepts and praises it if it is right. He may be unaware that certain pupils never take part in the recitation at all.

How does the teacher avoid the temptation of this kind of "discussion," either in his own or in the pupil's conditioning? For one thing, he keeps in mind a general direction for discussion. The direction is toward discussion in which all pupils bring to mind their own ideas so that they can contrast them with the insight from the story of faith. This does not mean that every pupil must say aloud what he thinks, but it does mean that every young person should think. Even this is not always possible. The junior high who has had a full Saturday and has gone to bed late may be too tired to think on Sunday. He may need to sit out the entire discussion or he may wake up later and join in.

Also, the direction toward thinking means that the teacher does not look for the pupil with the right answer, but for the pupil who is thinking and is ready to say something. He may or may not call on a pupil by name. When junior highs are unaccustomed to discussion, he may need to do so. "Do you have an idea, John?" he may ask, or, "What do you think, Mary?" Since John's and Mary's ideas are not the only possible ones, the teacher looks about for other pupils who are thinking. "Do you agree?" he may ask, or, "Who has another idea?"

Not all the answers given will be thoughtful ones. Some junior highs shrug off the challenge to think with, "I don't know." Occasionally a young person, called on to express an idea before he has thought it through, covers his unreadiness by clowning. The teacher's best procedure is to bypass such answers without comment and move on to someone else. But the teacher should know what the junior high is saying when he makes inappropriate answers. Perhaps it is, "I don't care"; "I'm too tired"; "You never give me time to say what I think"; "My idea will sound corny compared to Jim's"; or "I don't know what we're talking about."

Sometimes young people give "wild" answers that do not seem to make sense. Imagination carries them farther than the adult expects or than other young people can follow. In the discussion of Joseph, the boy who suggests that the brothers should have stayed home and worked the farm makes an error of fact and is corrected by the other pupils. The pupil who identifies radio preachers as crackpots (in study of Jesus' disciples) expresses an opinion on a matter not directly related to class discussion. Here it is the teacher who redirects discussion by turning back to a pupil who had spoken previously. Discussion of Paul's discovery elicits from one pupil an idea beyond the understanding of some members of the class. The teacher draws discussion back to a possibility that all can consider.

Frequently, but not always, the teacher *restates an answer* made by a young person. Wild answers can sometimes be salvaged in this way, provided the teacher is quick enough to grasp and interpret what the pupil meant. Other times the teacher restates in order to fill in gaps in the way a pupil expressed an idea and to make it clear to others. Or restatement may be used to carry an idea farther. In discussion of the medieval church, the teacher restates in a more general way the comment, "That way, what you mostly believe in is the priest, not God." The teacher rephrases and broadens the statement, "You don't really get to know someone on TV or in a newspaper article" (in the discussion of Jesus' disciples). It is well to use restatement sparingly and to avoid putting words in the mouths of the pupils. Junior highs become discouraged if everything they say is said over again in the teacher's words. The clue to whether restatement is necessary lies in how well the pupil's answer seems to be understood by others in the class. Sometimes it is better to ask the pupil himself to say what he meant or to allow time for other pupils to question him.

Another aspect of discussion appears here. It takes place *among all the persons in the class,* from pupil to pupil, from pupil to teacher, from teacher to pupil. Comments are not directed to the teacher or responded to only by him. The wise teacher deflects answers made directly to him, if the pupil is obviously "reciting" or trying to gain status by being right. In the study of Isaiah, the teacher turns aside such a comment ("That's what Jesus meant by 'turning the other cheek', isn't it?") by asking the pupil to think about his own question. On the other hand, in the discussion of the medieval church, the pupil who asks, "You mean if someone today told us what to believe and do, he might be wrong too?" is asking for clarification of the teacher's opinion. The teacher may or may not make an answer. In this case, another pupil speaks before the teacher can do so, which is probably all to the good. The teacher is saved from the temptation of expressing his own opinion at length, when he should express just so much of it as will elicit thought among the junior highs.

The teacher uses *additional questions* to carry discussion and thought farther, to draw it back into focus, to redirect it. Sometimes he restates the initial question or introduces it again in varied form. The teacher in the discussion of Isaiah refocuses thinking by asking the pupils to identify again the issue between the prophet and the people of God. The question represents a rephrasing of the initial question. In discussing Paul's discovery, the teacher varies the main question ("Do you want a set of rules given you on becoming a member of the church?"), and then gives an imaginary example, a Scout's promise and laws for church members.

Whereas the lead-off question is usually indicated in the teacher's material, he is often on his own when it comes to further questions. He makes them up on the spot, according to the direction in which the pupils seem to be thinking. Clues to what the young people think are not always answers or comments; there may be clues in facial expressions or even in silences. For example, the teacher in the discussion of Joseph decides on the spot to probe into the idea of goodies and baddies because he senses what the pupils are thinking but not saying. Discussion of Jesus' disciples takes a step toward further thinking when the teacher asks if firsthand knowing of Jesus Christ is possible today. The question was suggested in the teacher's material, but the teacher times its introduction partly on a hunch about one pupil's wistful desire to see Jesus Christ.

Sometimes the teacher asks *questions of the "tell us more" type* when a pupil's idea is not clearly expressed. "What do you mean?" asks the teacher of the pupil who sees that Joseph's dreams came true. "Explain," requests the teacher of the pupil who thinks God could use good people better (in the same discussion). The young person who exclaims, "That wasn't faith!" (in discussing the medieval church) is asked to say more. "Why did they have to?" the teacher asks of the pupil who says people in Isaiah's time had to trust in arms and alliances.

At other times the teacher *adds information* or directs the pupils to turn back to sources of information they have already explored. The latter is what the teacher does in directing the pupils to look up the references for Joseph's explanation. The teacher leading discussion of Paul's discovery introduces in middiscussion a technique of informal dramatization planned to help junior highs make use of what they have already learned. In discussing the medieval church the teacher gives information at two points. He reminds the pupils that the information they have does not show that medieval people rose up and overthrew the clergy. Then he adds information (that may or may not be new to the pupils) about the fact that some people did act secretly against the power of the church.

Many times the teacher consciously *encourages differences of opinion*. Some of these may be between pupils with different ideas. The girl who is certain that God punishes you is questioned by another pupil who sees little evidence of this (discussion of Joseph). In the discussion of the medieval church, one pupil says the Bible tells you what God wants you to do. Two other pupils express doubt about that opinion. The first pupil becomes too defensive, and the teacher directs discussion away from the question in order to prevent argument.

In both the study of the medieval church and in that of Isaiah, it is the teacher himself who keeps a differing idea before the young people. He does so because all or almost all the pupils are lined up on the side of one idea. In one case the pupils unanimously and somewhat shallowly believe that everyone always wants freedom. The teacher finally says he thinks people probably liked the authority of the clergy over them. Thus he puts another opinion over against the pupils' idea. The discussion of Isaiah requires the teacher to keep before the class a different idea from the one the young people hold almost exclusively. The teacher interprets the pupils' comments and suggests there might be a difference between saving a nation (what they want to do) and what God wanted his people to do.

The matter is one of more than a difference of opinion. It has to do with the contrast between insights from the story of faith and the present thoughts of the young people. "We found the Bible passage said so-and-so, which is different from what we think," is how a teacher might sum it up. But the means of highlighting the contrast may be by casting doubt on what the pupils are saying. "Is that true?" asks the teacher when the class says, "Everyone wants to be free," in study of the medieval church. Or it may be by saying, "You seem to think, but I think . . . ," or, flatly, "I don't agree with you," or, "Here is another way of thinking about it." In the discussion of Paul's discovery the possibility of another opposite, besides freedom to do anything you want, is suggested by reference to the apostle himself.

Finally there are points at which the teacher *summarizes what has been said* by the class. The teacher in the discussion of Isaiah summarizes in midstream in order to help the pupils see the similarities between their ideas and those of Isaiah's opponents. In the discussion of Paul's discovery, the teacher summarizes by writing on the chalkboard the main ideas that have been expressed. He does so to make clear to the pupils the question at which they have arrived ("What is it Christians are to do?"). The teacher in the discussion of the medieval church summarizes at the close of the session and suggests a question for further thought. The discussion of Isaiah ends with a summary also, in order to focus again on the contrast that has all along been difficult to maintain in the face of the pupils' ideas.

Study this section again. Make a list of the different kinds and uses of questions. What other functions of the teacher (besides asking questions) are suggested?

What is the difference between these two questions: The people of God had turned from trusting in God to trusting in arms and alliances, hadn't they? Why had God's people turned from trusting in him to trusting in arms and alliances?

What are the differences between the questions used by Teachers A and B, in the episodes at the beginning of the chapter, and the questions used in the demonstration discussions?

Many junior highs resent being encouraged to think in church school. Why do you think this is true? Often they will try to turn discussion into recitation. Why do you think they do so?

Do you believe young adolescents in general like to think? Do you feel they prefer the certainty of answers to their questions, and definite things to learn?

WHERE DISCUSSION COMES OUT

Discussion in study starts in thoughtfulness, proceeds in thoughtfulness, ends in thoughtfulness. Thinking is both its method and its aim.

For example, several of the demonstration discussions end with a thought question. The discussion of medieval faith leads to considering faith and authority. The teacher suggests two different ways for the junior highs to think about the difference between them.

Many teachers experience painful doubts, discomfort, even guilt, when a session with young people ends at such an inconclusive point. Instead of suggesting further thought, they feel compelled to come to a conclusion. In this case, the teacher is likely to cut off discussion and summarize with a definition of faith that he expects the pupils to comprehend, accept, and act upon.

Part of the teacher's compulsion is merely an adult preference for conclusions. Adults live in a world in which discussion comes to operative decisions. They are, so to speak, always acting like members of the board of managers, who discuss in order to come to decisions that are to be put into operation. Discussion about the family budget between husband and wife (the "members of the board"), when it doesn't become hopeless argument, results in decisions of what is to be done with money. Discussion among home builder, contractor, and builder results in understanding and application of a blue print so that a building can be constructed. In almost every case, discussion on the adult level comes to conclusions that can be put into effect in the practical world of work and everyday living.

The inner life of young adolescence, on the other hand, does not drive toward operative conclusions. How parents often wish it would! It tends to contemplate, to experiment, to compare ideas, to discard old ones, to take up new ones that will be compared with others, and perhaps discarded, perhaps retained. What adults regard as impractical about young people is precisely this quality of tentativeness. They almost always want to rush young people on to the way of thinking used in the "real," practical world in which decisions must be made. Not coming to conclusions can be painful for adults, and they suppose it must be equally painful for young pupils. Thus many teachers will say that it is not fair to leave junior highs up in the air without giving them answers.

Beyond the teacher's adult preference for practicality, is the pressure the church exerts on him to give the pupils answers. Nine tenths of the members of any church sincerely believe that the church's purpose in education is to get over its own point of view, The Faith. The teacher who feels he is under such pressure may allow thinking about faith versus authority to go on for a time. Then he might explain the Protestant idea of the priesthood of believers and expect the young people to accept it as the church's teaching on the question. Meantime, of course, the opportunity for thoughtfulness has been demolished, because authority has taken over, no matter how subtly it has used discussion to clear the way for its pronouncement.

Even the teacher who understands and believes that study must end in thoughtfulness and that faith is not conformity finds himself looking uneasily over his shoulder when he leaves young adolescents with questions instead of answers. The longer he proceeds in this direction, the more he finds that what he has fostered is an atmosphere of doubt. He may be delighted that junior highs feel free to question anything and to think things through. But he knows very well that the parents of the young people and most other members of his church would be dismayed. Doubt seems to be at the opposite pole from faith, because faith is commonly supposed to be belief and conviction, a tool of the practical world to be applied to life.

Teaching that comes to conclusions not only evades the inner life of young adolescents, it also evades faith. It turns away from the word of God that challenges the world in which adults and the church live comfortably. The conclusions it teaches are often escapes from the challenge of being confronted again and again with God's word to his people.

The final question about study is whether adults wish to think about, consider, and weigh insights from the story of faith along with young adolescents—or whether they prefer to pass on to young people the barriers against faith that they and the church have so carefully erected. Can teachers accept the challenge to study with young adolescents? Only teachers can say. It is fairly certain that junior highs are ready to do so.

If you are doubtful as to why study stops at the aim of thoughtfulness and sets forth no outcomes, reread Chapter 3.

How do you think parents and others in your church would react if they thought you were raising questions with junior highs and urging them to think, but not giving them answers?

As review, try defining in your own words what study is.